The Laurel Great Lives and Thought series is designed to present to the general reader and to students the best that has been expressed in the history of ideas, together with full-length portraits of the thinkers and doers whose contributions have left an indelible imprint upon the world's course.

The scope of the series is universal: every aspect of human experience—politics, history, sociology, religion, philosophy, psychology, science, literature, etc.—will receive its merited attention. The author-editors of THE GREAT LIVES AND THOUGHT are chosen both for their knowledge of the subject and for their ability to write lucidly.

Robert Bierstedt has been chairman of the All-University Department of Sociology and Anthropology at New York University since 1960. In 1959–60 he was a Fulbright lecturer at the University of Edinburgh, and gave the 1960 Barnett Lecture at Oxford University. He has also lectured at the universities of Southampton, Liverpool, and Munich. Professor Bierstedt is the author of THE SOCIAL ORDER, co-author of several books, including MODERN SOCIAL SCIENCE, and editor of THE MAKING OF SOCIETY.

Edgar Johnson, the General Editor, was formerly Chairman of the Department of English at City College of the City University of New York. He is the author of a definitive biography of Dickens and of ONE MIGHTY TORRENT: THE DRAMA OF BIOGRAPHY.

EMILE DURKHEIM

ROBERT BIERSTEDT

General Editor, Edgar Johnson

THE LAUREL GREAT LIVES AND THOUGHT

Published by Dell Publishing Co., Inc.
750 Third Avenue, New York, N. Y. 10017
Copyright © 1966 by Dell Publishing Co., Inc.
Laurel ® TM 674623, Dell Publishing Co., Inc.

First printing: January, 1966

Printed in the U. S. A.

Typography by R. Scudellari

ACKNOWLEDGMENTS: The selections in this volume are reproduced by permission of the following publishers:

from *The Division of Labor in Society* by Émile Durkheim.
Reprinted with permission of The Free Press of Glencoe.
Copyright 1933 by George Simpson.

from *The Rules of Sociological Method* by Émile Durkheim.
Reprinted with permission of The Free Press of Glencoe.
Copyright 1938 by The University of Chicago.

from *Suicide* by Émile Durkheim.
Reprinted with permission of the publisher.
Copyright 1951 by The Free Press, A Corporation.

from *Elementary Forms of Religious Life* by Émile Durkheim.
First published by The Free Press of Glencoe in 1954
and used with its permission and that of
George Allen & Unwin Ltd., London.

Contents

(Quotation marks indicate selections from Durkheim's writings.)

A Selective Bibliography

The following selections, by and about Durkheim, owe a great deal to the extensive bibliography prepared by Kurt H. Wolff and published in his *Emile Durkheim, 1858–1917* (Columbus, Ohio: Ohio State University Press, 1960). It has been necessary to add only a few items published since 1960. Durkheim's own works I have listed only in English translation but they are arranged in the chronological order of their original publication in French or, in the first case, Latin.

DURKHEIM'S WRITINGS

1892 *Montesquieu and Rousseau: Forerunners of Sociology*. Translated by Ralph Manheim, with a Foreword by Henri Peyre. Ann Arbor, Michigan: University of Michigan Press, 1960. (Contains Durkheim's Latin dissertation on Montesquieu.)

1893 *The Division of Labor in Society*. Translated and with an Introduction by George Simpson. New York: The Macmillan Company, 1933.

1895 *The Rules of Sociological Method*. Translated by Sarah A. Solovay and John H. Mueller, and edited by George E. G. Catlin. Chicago: University of Chicago Press, 1938.

1897 *Suicide: A Study in Sociology*. Translated by John A. Spaulding and George Simpson; edited and with an Introduction by George Simpson. Glencoe, Illinois: The Free Press of Glencoe, 1951.

Incest: The Nature and Origin of the Taboo. Translated and with an introduction by Edward Sagarin. New York: Lyle Stuart, Inc., 1963. Translation of "La Prohibition de l'Inceste et ses Origines," *l'Année Sociologique*, Vol. 1, No. 1, 1897.

1903 *Primitive Classification.* By Emile Durkheim and Marcel Mauss. Translated and with an Introduction by Rodney Needham. Chicago: University of Chicago Press, 1963. A translation of "De Quelques Formes Primitives de Classification," *l'Année Sociologique*, 1901–2 (1903).

1912 *The Elementary Forms of the Religious Life: A Study in Religious Sociology.* Translated by Joseph Ward Swain. London: Allen & Unwin, Ltd.; New York: The Macmillan Company, 1915.

1915 *Who Wanted War? The Origin of the War according to Diplomatic Documents.* Written in collaboration with E. Denis; translated by A. M. Wilson-Garinei. ("Studies and Documents on the War.") Paris: Armand Colin, 1915.

"Germany above All:" German Mentality and War. Translated by J. S. ("Studies and Documents on the War.") Paris: Armand Colin, 1915.

1922 *Education and Sociology.* Translated and with an Introduction by Sherwood D. Fox; Foreword by Talcott Parsons. Glencoe, Illinois: The Free Press of Glencoe, 1956.

1924 *Sociology and Philosophy.* Translated by D. F. Pocock and with an Introduction by J. G. Peristiany. Glencoe, Illinois: The Free Press of Glencoe, 1953.

1925 *Moral Education: A Study in the Theory and Application of the Sociology of Education.* Translated by Everett K. Wilson and Herman Schnurer. Edited and with an Introduction by Everett K. Wilson; Foreword by Paul Fauconnet. New York: The Free Press of Glencoe, Inc., 1961.

1928 *Socialism and Saint-Simon.* Translated by Charlotte Sattler. Edited and with an Introduction by Alvin W. Gouldner. Yellow Springs, Ohio: Antioch Press, 1958.

1950 *Professional Ethics and Civic Morals.* Translated by Cornelia Brookfield, and with a Preface by H. Nail Kubali and an Introduction by Georges Davy. London: Routledge & Kegan Paul, Ltd., 1957.

1955 *Pragmatism and Sociology.* (First, second, third, fourth, fifth, thirteenth, and fourteenth lectures delivered at the Sorbonne in 1913–14). Constituted from the notes of students by Armand Cuvillier and translated by Charles Blend. In *Emile Durkheim, 1858–1917,* edited by Kurt H. Wolff. Columbus, Ohio: The Ohio State University Press, 1960, pp. 386–436.

WRITINGS ABOUT DURKHEIM

1895 Sorel, Georges. "Les théories de M. Durkheim." *Le devenir social,* I (1895), pp. 1–26, 148–80.

1896 Tufts, James H. "Recent Sociological Tendencies in France." *American Journal of Sociology,* I (1896), pp. 446–56.

1897 Barth, Paul. *Die Philosophie der Geschichte als Soziologie.* 4th Edition. Leipzig: O. R. Reisland, 1922. Vol. I, pp. 628–42.

1898 Belot, Gustave. "Emile Durkheim: L'Année sociologique." *Revue philosophique,* XLV (1898), pp. 649–57.

Tosti, Gustavo. "Suicide in the Light of Recent Studies." *American Journal of Sociology,* III (1898), pp. 464–78.

Tosti, Gustavo. "The Delusions of Durkheim's Sociological Objectivism." *American Journal of Sociology,* IV (1898), pp. 171–77.

1911 Davy, Georges. "La sociologie de M. Durkheim." *Revue philosophique,* LXXII (1911), pp. 42–71, 160–85.

1914 Wallis, Wilson D. "Durkheim's View of Religion." *Journal of Religious Psychology,* VII (1914), pp. 252–67.

1915 Gehlke, Charles Elmer. *Emile Durkheim's Contributions to Sociological Theory.* ("Studies in History, Economics and Public Law," No. 151.) New York: Columbia University Press, 1915.

1917 Goldenweiser, Alexander A. "Religion and Society: A Critique of Durkheim's Theory of the Origin and Nature of Religion" (1917). *History, Psy-*

chology and Culture. New York: Alfred A. Knopf, 1933, Part IV, Chap. i, pp. 361–73.

Worms, René. "Emile Durkheim," *Revue internationale de sociologie,* XXV (1917), pp. 561–68.

1918 Branford, Victor. "Durkheim: A Brief Memoir." *Sociological Review,* X (1918), pp. 77–82.

Halbwachs, Maurice. "La doctrine d'Emile Durkheim." *Revue philosophique,* LXXXV (1918), pp. 353–411.

Lenoir, Raymond. "Emile Durkheim et la conscience moderne." *Mercure de France,* CXXVII (1918), pp. 577–95.

Pécaut, Félix. "Emile Durkheim." *Revue pédagogique,* Nouvelle Série, LXXII (1918), pp. 1–20.

1919 Parodi, Dominique. "Emile Durkheim et l'école sociologique" (Chap. v). *La philosophie contemporaine en France: Essai de classification des doctrines.* 2nd rev. ed. Paris: Félix Alcan, 1920, pp. 113–60.

1919–1920 Davy, Georges. "Emile Durkheim," *Revue de métaphysique et de morale,* XXVI (1919), pp. 181–98; XXVII (1920), pp. 71–112.

1920 Barnes, Harry Elmer. "Durkheim's Contribution to the Reconstruction of Political Theory." *Political Science Quarterly,* XXXV (1920), pp. 236–54.

Schaub, Edward. "A Sociological Theory of Knowledge." *Philosophical Review,* XXIX (1920), pp. 319–39.

1922 Fauconnet, Paul. "The Pedagogical Work of Emile Durkheim." *American Journal of Sociology,* XXVIII (1922), pp. 529–53.

1923 Mauss, Marcel. "In memoriam: L'Oeuvre inédite de Durkheim et de ses collaborateurs." *l'Année sociologique,* Nouvelle Série, I (1923), pp. 7–29.

1924 Dennes, William Ray. "Durkheim" (Chap. iii). *The Method and Presuppositions of Group Psychology* ("University of California Publications in Philosophy," No. 6). Berkeley and Los Angeles: University of California Press, 1924.

1926 Lacombe, Roger. *La méthode sociologique de Durkheim: Etude critique.* Paris: Félix Alcan, 1926.

Perry, Ralph Barton, *General Theory of Value.* New York: Longmans, Green & Co., Inc., 1926, Chaps.

xiv–xvii, pp. 400–519.

1927 Fauconnet, Paul. "The Durkheim School in France." *Sociological Review*, XIX (1927), pp. 15–20.

1928 Sorokin, Pitirim. *Contemporary Sociological Theories*. New York and London: Harper & Bros., 1928, Chap. viii, pp. 463–80.

1930 Bouglé, Célestin; Davy, Georges; Granet, Marcel; Lenoir, Raymond; and Maublanc, René. "L'oeuvre sociologique d'Emile Durkheim." *Europe*, XXII (1930), pp. 281–304.

Richard, Gaston. "La pathologie sociale d'Emile Durkheim," *Revue internationale de sociologie*, XXXVIII (1930), pp. 113–26.

1931 Mitchell, Marion M. "Emile Durkheim and the Philosophy of Nationalism." *Political Science Quarterly*, XLVI (1931), pp. 87–106.

1932 Marica, George M. *Emile Durkheim: Soziologie und Soziologismus*. Jena: Gustav Fischer, 1932.

1933 Simpson, George. Emile Durkheim's Social Realism." *Sociology and Social Research*, XVIII (1933), pp. 3–11.

1934 Merton, Robert K. "Durkheim's Division of Labor in Society." *American Journal of Sociology*, XL (1934), pp. 319–28.

1937 Gurvitch, Georges, "La science des faits moraux et la morale théorique chez Emile Durkheim." *Archives de philosophie du droit et de sociologie juridique*, VII (1937), pp. 18–44.

Marjolin, Robert. "French Sociology: Comte and Durkheim," translated by Alice Price Duncan and Hugh Dalziel Duncan. *American Journal of Sociology*, XLII (1937), pp. 693–704, 901–2.

Parsons, Talcott. *The Structure of Social Action*. New York and London: McGraw-Hill Book Company, 1937, Chaps. viii–xii, pp. 301–470.

1938 Barnes, Harry Elmer, and Becker, Howard. *Social Thought from Lore to Science*. Washington D.C.: Harren Press, 1952, Vol. II, Chap. xxii, pp. 829–39.

1939 Alpert, Harry. *Emile Durkheim and His Sociology*. New York: Columbia University Press, 1939.

1943 DeGré, Gerard L. *Society and Ideology: An Inquiry into the Sociology of Knowledge*. New York: Columbia University Bookstore, 1943, Chap. iii, pp.

54–84.

1945 Lévi-Strauss, Claude. "French Sociology" (Chap. xvii), in *Twentieth Century Sociology,* edited by Georges Gurvitch and Wilbert E. Moore. New York: Philosophical Library, 1945.

1948 Benoit-Smullyan, Emile. "The Sociologism of Emile Durkheim and His School," (Chap. xxvii), in *An Introduction to the History of Sociology,* edited by Harry Elmer Barnes. Chicago: University of Chicago Press, 1948.

1950 Simpson, George, "Methodological Problems in Determining the Aetiology of Suicide." *American Sociological Review,* XVI (1950), pp. 658–63.

1951 Ginsberg, Morris. "Durkheim's Ethical Theory" (Chap. iv), *On the Diversity of Morals.* New York: The Macmillan Company, 1957, pp. 41–53.

1955 Friedmann, Georges, "La thèse de Durkheim et les formes contemporaines de la division du travail." *Cahiers internationaux de sociologie,* XIX (1955), pp. 45–58.

Ginsberg, Morris. "Durkheim's Theory of Religion" (Chap. xiv), *On the Diversity of Morals.* New York: The Macmillan Company, 1957, pp. 230–42.

Koseki, Toichiro. "Social Factors in E. Durkheim's Theory." *Japanese Sociological Review,* VI (1955), pp. 51–67.

Ottaway, A. K. C. "The Educational Sociology of Emile Durkheim." *British Journal of Sociology,* VI (1955), pp. 213–27.

1956 Worsley, P. M. "Emile Durkheim's Theory of Knowledge." *Sociological Review,* IV, New Series (1956), pp. 47–62.

1958 *American Journal of Sociology,* LXII (May, 1958), "Durkheim-Simmel Commemorative Issue."

Rossi, Peter H. "Emile Durkheim and Georg Simmel," p. 579.

Naegele, Kaspar D. "Attachment and Alienation: Complementary Aspects of the Work of Durkheim and Simmel," pp. 580–89.

Wolff, Kurt H. "The Challenge of Durkheim and Simmel," pp. 590–96.

Selvin, Hanan C. "Durkheim's *Suicide* and Problems of Empirical Research," pp. 607–19.

Schnore, Leo F. "Social Morphology and Human Ecology," pp. 620–34.

Gold, Martin. "Suicide, Homicide, and the Socialization of Aggression," pp. 561–61.

Alpert, Harry. "Emile Durkheim: Enemy of Fixed Psychological Elements," pp. 662–64.

Spencer, Robert F. "Culture Process and Intellectual Current: Durkheim and Ataturk." *American Anthropologist*, LX (1958), pp. 640–57.

1959 Alpert, Harry. "Emile Durkheim: A Perspective and Appreciation." *American Sociological Review*, XXIV (1959), pp. 462–65.

Bellah, Robert N. "Durkheim and History." *American Sociological Review*, XXIV (1959), pp. 447–61.

Dohrenwend, Bruce P. "Egoism, Altruism, Anomie: A Conceptual Analysis of Durkheim's Types." *American Sociological Review*, XXIV (1959), pp. 466–72.

1960 Davy, Georges. "Emile Durkheim." *Revue française de sociologie*, I (1960), pp. 3–24.

Wolff, Kurt H. (ed.). *Emile Durkheim, 1858–1917*. Columbus, Ohio: The Ohio State University Press, 1960.

1962 Edward A. Tiryakian. *Sociologism and Existentialism: Two Perspectives on the Individual and Society*. Englewood Cliffs, N. J.: Prentice-Hall, Inc., 1962.

1964 Wolff, Kurt H. (ed.). *Essays on Sociology and Philosophy*, by Emile Durkheim *et al.* (Harper Torchbooks) New York, Evanston, and London: Harper & Row, 1964.

1965 Nisbet, Robert A. *Emile Durkheim* (with selected essays). Englewood Cliffs, N. J.: Prentice-Hall, Inc., 1965.

THE
part 1 LIFE OF
DURKHEIM

Émile Durkheim was born on April 15, 1858 in the small town of Épinal in the low foothills of the Vosges Mountains, which form the western slope of the valley of the Rhine in northeastern France. The region is part of the plain of Lorraine, which includes such larger cities as Nancy and Strasbourg, and it is one that has contributed other distinguished sons as well to the culture and politics of France.

For centuries this countryside, then and later a battlefield, had been the ancestral locus of generations of industrious artisans and peasants, far removed from the more indolent, Latin influences of the maritime provinces on the Mediterranean. The region had still another characteristic: it contained, with complete toleration, more Frenchmen of the Jewish faith than any other part of the country. Durkheim himself was born of Jewish parents, a descendant of rabbis and rabbinical scholars, and, at an age when other children are still enjoying a carefree playtime, he had already dedicated himself to the rabbinate.

The dedication, however, was destined to be short-lived. Under the influence of one of his teachers, a woman of the Catholic faith, the young Durkheim had some kind of a mystical experience, the details of which are unknown, and he emerged from it an agnostic, a position he was to retain for the remainder of his life. He had not been denied, however, some early Hebrew instruction and this fact doubtless had something to do with the erudition he was able to bring to his later studies of religion. His early encounters with religion, both Jewish and Catholic, also had something to do, or so one may suppose, with his constant preoccupation with problems of ethical significance. There was always in his personality, in addition, something of the apostle and the prophet, something that transcended a purely intellectual interest in the sociology of religion.

Persons who are destined to become eminent professors usually receive their first distinction in their earliest education, and Durkheim was no exception. He was advanced rapidly in his elementary and secondary schools and had no difficulty winning prizes for superior achievement. Upon receiving his baccalaureate—or, rather, two baccalaureates—from the *collège* of his native town, he was already determined to pursue an academic career and, indeed, his prospects were brilliant. He thought of his future, as his biographer Georges Davy reminds us, as one involving not only teaching and learning but also as one that would involve both his students and himself in the social amelioration of France.

In his little book on Durkheim, Davy reproduces a photograph of the young man taken when he was a student at the local college. Harry Alpert remarks about this photograph as follows:

The photograph is not very clear, but in it we perceive the bright youngster as he rests his left arm on the shoulder of a comrade. His high forehead is surrounded by very thick hair which is especially bushy at the sides. The facial features reveal an almost feminine delicacy and sensitivity; a keen intelligence is unmistakably manifested in the boy's visage. The delicate hand we see seems, as it droops from the wrist, to end in unusually long fingers. This sensitiveness of feature and mien remained with Durkheim throughout his life.*

*Harry Alpert, *Émile Durkheim and His Sociology* (New York: Russell & Russell, Inc., 1961), p. 16.

His attitude, however, even at this early age, was serious, his demeanor grave. Already he entertained the conviction that life does not necessarily offer either pleasure or happiness but only the opportunity to learn from various episodes of grief and misfortune.

Upon graduation from his college at Épinal, the young Durkheim, having won national honors in the competition for the École Normale Supérieure, went to Paris to prepare himself for this famous academy. Those who were admitted to it and who passed its course of instruction were qualified to hold posts for life in the French educational system. Already Durkheim had won a degree of security, and already he had taken the first steps in a career that was to lead him to a professorship.

In Paris, however, these initial steps were not destined to be easy ones. Although none of the biographers has any ready explanation, Durkheim was not successful in winning admittance to the École Normale on his first attempt. Nor, indeed, was he on the second attempt. It was only in the third year at the Lycée Louis-le-Grand, the preparatory school, that he passed the required tests. It appears that there was something in the purely humanistic spirit in which French, Latin, Greek, philosophy, and history were taught at the Lycée that failed to inspire the young student. One might put it more positively and say that a purely literary humanism was foreign to the more positivistic and scientific attitudes that, from whatever source, had already won lodgment in his mind.

In any event, he became in 1879, at the age of twenty-one, a student in good standing at the École Normale. Salomon Reinach, the archeologist, and Lucien Lévy-Bruhl, the anthropologist, had just been graduated; Henri Bergson, to become the most distinguished French philosopher of his era, had been admitted the year before, along with Jean Léon Jaurès, whom philosophy had later to surrender to politics; and in Durkheim's own class were such figures as Pierre Janet, the psychologist; Goblot, the logician; and still others who were to achieve eminence in various fields of scholarship and of learning. Among the students at the school at that time or later who were to win fame as sociologists, we find the names of Alfred Espinas, Jean Izoulet, Henri Berr, Célestin Bouglé, Henri Hubert, François Simiand, Marcel Granet, and Georges Davy.

Durkheim's student years, however, were not as happy as they might have been. He confronted at the École Normale the same humanistic emphasis that had earlier caused him some discomfiture and that was, from other vantages, one of the distinctive merits of the French educational process. Latin verse and Greek prose, which were the staples of his intellectual diet, did not seem to him to meet the challenges of the time, and accordingly he chafed under the regimen of his classes and assignments. In his account of the situation, Henri Peyre refers to the German chemist, Wilhelm Ostwald, who said that one of the surest signs of future greatness in a student is his rebellion against his teachers.* Certainly Durkheim was in rebellion at the École Normale—as, incidentally, Auguste Comte was against *his* teachers a generation earlier. In any event, neither the regimen nor the rebellion did any permanent damage, and in later years Durkheim remembered his old school with affection, as most of us tend to do, and indeed recalled many happy occasions with his classmates. When it came time for his son, André, to choose his vocation, he too went to the École Normale.

We know also that Durkheim won the approval even of some of the teachers from whom he withheld his total admiration, and that one instructor, Delacoulonche, read to the entire class an essay that Durkheim had written on Schiller. The subject of another of his papers

*Henri Peyre, "Durkheim: The Man, His Time, and His Intellectual Background," in *Émile Durkheim, 1858–1917* edited by Kurt H. Wolff (Columbus: The Ohio State University Press, 1960), p. 9.

was the Jews in the Roman Empire. In his classes and with his classmates, Durkheim spoke often and eloquently, and argued with passion the literary, philosophical, and political issues of the day. As Davy tells us, Durkheim spoke "abundantly," often without notes, and with a "passionate ardor and imperious decision." At one point he gave an extemporaneous talk on Molière that astonished his listeners with its originality and brilliance. At the same time he retained his solemnity and approached each task with an austerity his classmates may not have regarded as commensurate with its difficulty. They gave him a sobriquet—The Metaphysician—and remarked on his "precocious maturity."

However much one may value a hard discipline in language, literature, and philosophy, it remains true that the École Normale was hostile to outside influences, and, during the time of his attendance there, Durkheim received little notion of the scientific developments occurring elsewhere in France and in other countries. It was only after he was graduated, for example, that he learned of the work of such eminent psychologists as Charcot and Ribot and, in Germany, Wilhelm Wundt. It was probably in his second year, however, that he became acquainted with the work of Renouvier and Comte, and these two, philosopher and sociologist respectively (at that time a distinction without a difference), were among the most important of the intellectual influences to which he was exposed. It was in his second year too that Durkheim wrote an essay on "The I," or the Self, which attracted the attention of the philosopher Émile Boutroux, who thereupon invited Durkheim to write his doctoral dissertation under his supervision—an invitation, incidentally, that was an accolade of a rather rare order.

Boutroux's interest in his student was well reciprocated. It was from his teachings that Durkheim imbibed some of the principles and doctrines that he was to express later on in his own work. Among these doctrines was a distrust of atomism and of reductionism and a belief that something new always emerges in a synthesis and that this cannot be wholly explained by analysis of its constituent parts. Phenomena always have to be explained on their own level, in terms pertaining to their own kind, and not on some lower, more elementary or more fundamental level. Thus, already we see the germ of Durkheim's insistence that social facts can be explained only by other social facts, and not by psychological or biological facts. And we see also the germ of the notion that society is a reality *sui generis,* something that has to be explained in its own terms and not in terms that are taken from any other science. The sciences themselves are independent and autonomous and each has its own level of operation, its own mode of explanation. These ideas can be found in Boutroux's books. It was Boutroux also who suggested to Durkheim that he write his thesis on Montesquieu, and it was to Boutroux that Durkheim later dedicated his book *The Division of Labor in Society: "A mon cher maître M. Émile Boutroux: Hommage réspectueux et réconnaissant."*

One would be remiss, in mentioning Durkheim's teachers, to omit the name of Fustel de Coulanges, author of *The Ancient City,* and a critical and positivistically inclined historian, who became Director of the School in 1880 and who was able to modify its curricular policies in directions that were more congenial to his student's views. It was to his memory that Durkheim dedicated his Latin thesis on Montesquieu.

One does not like to mention it and yet it must nevertheless be said that, during these undergraduate years at the École Normale Durkheim was a bit of a prig so far as his relations both with his teachers and with his associates were concerned. He was altogether serious; he detested the light touch; there seems to have been no humor in him and, what is worse, no breath of tolerance for those—superiors and companions alike—whose views and whose temperaments differed from his own. His mien was altogether somber, his severity unleavened, his commitment total. These traits of personality limited somewhat the circle of those he admitted to friendship and doubtless limited also influences of a more comprehensive kind that could have rounded his character and smoothed its rougher contours. This is not to say, of course, that he lacked friends. Indeed, for several of his classmates he preserved a deep affection throughout his life. He enjoyed the normal conversational polemics with his associates and engaged in most of the political battles that agitate the minds of the most capable students in any era of history and in any country of the world. Durkheim, furthermore, felt that any philosophy that was devoid of political implications was a poor and forlorn thing, hardly worth the study, and that, in addition, every political position required a philosophical justification. And already it was that part of philosophy known then as sociology which lay at the very foundation of this justification.

It must not be supposed, however, that Durkheim, studious as he was, was also a recluse. We have it on good evidence that, during his years at the École Normale, he celebrated the 14th of July in the streets with the rest of the Parisian crowd and enjoyed the excitement that has always characterized that crowd from the first 14th to the present. Durkheim, in short, had pleasures as well as problems during his years at school.

In his third year his progress was interrupted by a serious illness, an attack of erysipelas, sometimes known as St. Anthony's fire, a painful eruption of the skin accompanied by fever and listlessness—and, of all the ills of the flesh, listlessness is the one that the scholar can least accommodate. As a final token of his difficulties with what he regarded as the philosophical superficiality and literary dilettantism of the École Normale, it should be recorded, perhaps, that, when he took his *agrégation* in 1882, his name was next to last on the list of the successful candidates.

After his graduation Durkheim spent the next five years, from 1882 to 1887, with one interval, as a teacher of philosophy in three provincial high schools near Paris—Sens, Saint-Quentin, and Troyes. Since philosophy may seem a rather recondite subject to be found in the high-school curriculum, it should be said that it plays a central role in the French educational system. Indeed, pupils in what corresponds to the fifth grade in the elementary school in the United States are already reading and studying Descartes' *Essay on Method*. In addition, the last year of the *lycée* in France is devoted entirely to philosophy for students who are "majoring," as we say, in the humanities, and their studies include, therefore, psychology, logic, ethics, metaphysics, and the history of philosophy. It was almost entirely due to Durkheim's influence that sociology was later added to this curriculum, as a necessary accompaniment of ethics.

The teaching experience was a rewarding one for Durkheim. He had no difficulty in capturing the imagination of his seventeen-year-old pupils as he guided them through the traditional problems of philosophy— the mind-body problem, the problem of the freedom of the will, the problem of the nature of reality, the problem of knowledge—which have agitated restless minds from the very beginning of civilization, problems, too, that continue to provide a common fund and a common foundation for all the nations of the West. Durkheim, then and later, was a dedicated teacher. Unlike some of the university teachers of today, who, in the passion for pure research, sometimes regard students as, at best, necessary evils and, at worst, unpleasant nuisances, Durkheim always regarded his teaching obligations with the utmost seriousness, both in the *lycée* and at the university.

His seriousness was a partner of his success. Indeed,

Durkheim became one of the great teachers in the history of French education. His lectures were carefully planned in advance, often written verbatim, and always clear and cogent. The scope of his learning and the sheer mastery of his subject matter entranced and enchanted those who were fortunate enough to sit in his classes. They came to respect above all the power of his reasoning, which, in a Frenchman, is the highest accolade of all. All universities have their great teachers, names that retain their luster through many generations of students. Durkheim's belongs among them, and belongs, too, to that smaller circle of those who combine a superior pedagogy with distinguished contributions to their chosen field of inquiry.

During the academic term 1885-1886, Durkheim took a year's leave of absence from his teaching duties in order to devote himself to further study. The first half of the year he spent in Paris and the second half in Germany. He went to Germany especially to explore the state of philosophical instruction in that country, especially of instruction in ethics. He was naturally interested also in the state of social science, a subject then still considered, in Germany, as elsewhere, a part of philosophy. Much of the German sojourn was spent in Berlin and Leipzig, and in the latter city he was especially attracted by the work of Wundt, who had founded the first psychological laboratory in the world and who proposed to apply scientific methods to the study of the mind. This was an exciting development for the young Durkheim and one that stimulated him to strive for the same kind of precision and objectivity in the study of society. He seems to have been less impressed by the German Spencerian Albert Schäffle, although his first published work, in 1885, was a review of Schäffle's *Bau und Leben des Sozialen Körpers*. The two reports that he wrote on the year's activities, one on philosophical instruction in general and the other on the new positive science of ethics, immediately made a reputation for him in France and led directly to the last of his days in the *lycée* and the beginning of his university career.

In the year 1887 a course in social science was created especially for Durkheim at the University of Bordeaux and it was to that city that he repaired. Nine years later, in 1896, he won his chair. It was the first professorship in social science in France. The years at Bordeaux were a most fruitful period. During this time he published three of his four most important books, *The Division of Labor in Society* in 1893, *The Rules of Sociological Method* in 1895, and *Suicide* in 1897. The fourth one, *The Elementary Forms of the Religious Life,* did not appear until 1912.

Among the courses that Durkheim offered at Bordeaux were Social Solidarity, Sociology of the Family, Suicide, Criminal Sociology, Pedagogy in the Nineteenth Century, Psychology Applied to Education, Religion, The History of Socialist Doctrines in France, Punishment and Responsibility, The Social Organization of Primitive Australian Societies, The History of Sociological Doctrines, and two with the curious titles Physiology of Law and Ethics, and General Physics of Ethics and Law. It is easy to read his intellectual interests in the titles of these courses and indeed they reflect in addition the research and writing in which he was engaged. The course in religion, whatever its effect on his students, had an interesting effect on the instructor. As an agnostic Durkheim had been inclined to denigrate the importance of religion in human life and society. When he began to develop his course, however, he discovered that, sociologically at least, religion was much more important than he had thought. Although his agnosticism was unaffected, then or later, he nevertheless wrote the following:

It was only in 1895 that I had a clear understanding of the capital role played by religion in social life. It was in that year that, for the first time, I found the means of approaching the study of religion sociologically. It was a revelation to me. The course of 1895 marks a line of demarcation in the development of my thought; so much so, that all my previous researches had to be taken up again with renewed efforts in order to be placed in harmony with these new views.*

By this time Durkheim had begun to publish extensively in the learned journals, and in 1898 he founded a new sociological periodical, *L'Année sociologique,* of which he was the editor for twelve years, until 1910. It was around this periodical that he figuratively gathered his friends and disciples and it was through the journal that he was able to exercise so large an influence not only on the development of French sociology but on French intellectual history in general. He gave direction and caliber to the journal, and the journal in turn gave status and repute to the science of sociology in France. These, of course, are only external facts about a new journal of a learned group. What his views were about the science that the journal celebrated and advanced we shall see in another section of this book. The group was so closely knit together, however, that Davy is able to refer to *"une petite société* sui generis, *le clan de l'-Année sociologique."* Durkheim created and maintained the spirit and the unity of this *"petite* society" and he did this without a *soupçon* of authoritarianism as he encouraged each of his followers to frame their own opinions and to publish them in its pages. The intellectual community that he had thus created, and to which we shall refer again, was in fact one of the three "schools" of sociology that have appeared so far in the history of the discipline, the other two being the Polish school of Znaniecki and the truly remarkable Chicago school (including, for a time, Znaniecki), which was founded by Albion W. Small before the turn of the

*Quoted by Harry Alpert, *op. cit.,* p. 67.

century and which flourished at least until the middle of
the second quarter of the same century.

The influence of the *Année* was a reciprocal one, as
these influences almost inevitably are. The journal, in
fact, played a decisive role in the development of Durkheim's thought. The labor was heavy, as any contemporary editor will readily testify, its rewards were few,
but there is something about the discipline involved that
hones the mind and sharpens its faculty as an instrument in the pursuit of knowledge. Durkheim's editor-
ship of the *Année,* and the fruitful collaboration this
post made possible with his disciples, could be a subject
for a doctoral dissertation, significant both in the explanation of Durkheim and as a contribution to the history
of sociology.

Very little is known, unfortunately, about the details
of Durkheim's family life. Around the time of his appointment at Bordeaux, he married Louise Dreyfus and
they had two children, Marie and André. His wife apparently shared without stint his editorial duties, reliev-
ing him of many of the chores of copyreading, proof-
reading, correspondence, and the like, and made it
possible for him thus to devote a larger amount of always limited time to the writing of his own books and
articles. The biographers are silent on the details of his
wife's family, but she was not related to Captain Alfred
Dreyfus, who lived from 1859 to 1935. Although not
one of the leaders of the liberal faction, Durkheim nevertheless played a part in the famous Dreyfus Affair
and served as a volunteer in the so-called Army of Justice. The fact is less important now perhaps for what it
is than for what it suggests, namely, that Durkheim accepted the responsibilities of citizenship as well as those
of scholarship and did not hesitate to speak out when
the occasion demanded it.

In the year 1902, fifteen years after his appointment
at Bordeaux, Durkheim was called to the University of
Paris to substitute for a year for a professor of educa-

tion, Buisson, who had been elected to the Chamber of Deputies. Four years later, in 1906, Durkheim succeeded to Buisson's chair. It is worth a remark that even at this late date Durkheim, in spite of the eminence that his work had earned him, was given a chair in education and not in sociology. It was a measure of the distrust of sociology that still obtained at the Sorbonne. It was not until 1913, four years before his death, that the title of the chair was changed to "Science of Education and Sociology," and a special decree was required to do it. It was the first time that the word "sociology" was attached to an academic chair in France. (Even then France was ahead of England in this respect, though far behind Germany and the United States.)

The courses that Durkheim taught at Paris include, among others, Moral Education, The History of Secondary Instruction in France, Ethics, The Origin of Religion, The Evolution of Marriage and the Family, The History of Pedagogic Doctrines, Moral Education in the School, Pragmatism and Sociology, Theoretical and Civic Ethics, The Social Philosophy of Comte and Saint Simon, and Great Pedagogical Doctrines of the Eighteenth and Nineteenth Centuries.* In all of these courses he exhibited his brilliance as a teacher. Those who were privileged to hear him were impressed by the organization of his lectures (often written), by the eloquence of his delivery, and by the profundity and scope of his concerns. One of his students indeed was to compare him, in an essay, with such heroes of human thought as Aristotle, Descartes, Spinoza, and Kant.

Most of Durkheim's energies during his first years at the Sorbonne were consumed in the expansion of his ideas, the writing of his books, and the teaching of his courses. He was not in the center of the conflicts that agitated the Sorbonne of that day, a battle of the books in which classicist found himself arrayed against mod-

*The course titles, both at Bordeaux and at Paris, are from Alpert, *op. cit.*, pp. 64–66.

ernist in intellectual activity, and Royalist against Socialist in the political arena. He continued instead to work
on the sociological journal that he had founded and
made one of the greatest of the learned journals. There
are those who will say that the *Année sociologique* not
only instituted and established a science of sociology in
France but that it transformed the basic premises of
several of the other learned disciplines as well.

Some cogency can be attached to this observation.
To do so one need only call the roll of Durkheim's col-
laborators who contributed papers during this period:
Georges Davy, Georges Scelle, Marcel Mauss, and
Maurice Hauriou in the sociology of law; Hubert Bour-
gin and François Simiand in economics; Lucien Febvre
and Roger Dion in history and geography; Henry Hubert in archeology; Marcel Granet in Sinology (whose
great book *La Pensée chinoise* is required reading in
sociology); Antoine Meillet, De Saussure, and
Benvenisté in linguistics; Claude Lévy-Strauss and
Roger Caillois in anthropology; Louis Hourticq in the
history of art; and Maurice Halbwachs, who continued
Durkheim's own studies in the field of suicide and who
wrote on the social context of memory. Halbwachs and
Mauss, the latter Durkheim's nephew, take first rank
among those who shared Durkheim's interests and who
continued his work after the master's death.* These are
the men who constituted what we have called the Durkheim school. It is a distinguished list and one that
gives testimony to the brilliance of sociological thought
in France.

The last years of Durkheim's life were destined to
differ from those of the earlier and quieter decade. Like
other Frenchmen, and Europeans generally, he was
caught up in the turbulence of World War I, and
devoted most of his hours to the service of his country.
When the Germans issued a manifesto defending the

---

*Halbwachs, Jewish like Durkheim, was killed in Buchenwald in
1945.

war and approving the invasion of Belgium, the German intellectuals were swept along in agreement and indeed feared the consequences of doing otherwise. The French replied. Among these replies was a volume on French science (*La science française,* 1915) that was sponsored by the French Ministry of Education and that contained chapters by both Durkheim and Bergson, among others. Durkheim wrote at least two pamphlets—*Qui a voulu la guerre?* and *L'Allemagne au-dessus de tout (Deutschland über Alles)*—in which he fixed the blame for the war on Germany and discussed at length the kind of psychology that would support the sentiment expressed in the second of these titles. In the second of these pamphlets he was especially critical of the Prussian historian, Heinrich von Treitschke (1834-1896), who expressed in his writings an extreme pan-Germanism.

Durkheim also served as secretary for the Committee for the Publication of Studies and Documents on the War—along with other scholars, scientists, and philosophers—and had something to do with one of the Committee's publications entitled *Lettres à tous les Français,* which was designed to repair morale and restore patriotic fervor during the series of military disasters encountered on the Eastern Front in 1915. Alpert credits Durkheim with having coined the motto "Patience, Effort, Confidence," which accomplished for the French at that time what the words of Winston Churchill were to accomplish for the British in another war at another time. Durkheim also served on numerous committees, including the Council of the University of Paris, and others on Franco-American Fraternity, University Rapprochement, For the Jews in Neutral Countries, and The Republican League of Alsace-Lorraine.

The war brought, in addition, a personal tragedy from which Durkheim never recovered. It was not enough that more than half of the students who had entered the École Normale in 1913 were killed before the war was over. Eighteen members of the class of 1911 were killed or wounded in a single action—the retreat from Serbia. Among these latter was Durkheim's son André, who died in a Bulgarian hospital just before Christmas of 1915. Although he bore his loss with Stoicism, Durkheim's friends began to notice that he was no longer his old and energetic self. André had been very close to him, both son and disciple, and he was already a promising student of linguistics. Durkheim tried to keep his grief within himself, discouraged any mention of it among his friends, and went his way. The strain, however, was too much. In December of 1916 he fell ill and less than a year later he was dead. He had gone to Fontainebleau for the summer of 1917 and hoped, while there, to write his book on ethics. The date of his death was November 15, 1917, his age fifty-nine.

The preceding account of Durkheim's life has sketched only its externals, as it were, and has neglected entirely the development of his ideas, a task reserved for the remainder of this book. It seems appropriate to add a word here, however, again of external detail, about his writings and the order in which they were published.

We have already mentioned his first published review —of a book by Schäffle—which appeared in 1885, his twenty-seventh year. The same year produced reviews also of books by Fouillée and Gumplowicz and the following year the two reports on German philosophical instruction, which we have mentioned. Durkheim continued to write reviews in the years immediately following, and the authors represented are Spencer, Coste, DeGréef, Guyau, and Tönnies, all of whom were prominent names in the rising discipline of sociology. All these, however, were prior to the publication of his own first books. Afterwards, and throughout his career, he wrote many more reviews.

Although it may seem like cruel and inhuman treatment to the graduate student of today, who regards his course of study as one formidable obstacle after another, the student of Durkheim's day at the École Normale had to write not one but two theses, one in French and the other in Latin. Durkheim's Latin dissertation was on Montesquieu and was published in Bordeaux in 1892 under the title *Quid secundatus politicae scientiae instituendae contulerit*. In this thesis Durkheim gave Montesquieu credit for first realizing the possibility of a social science and for trying to bring the discrete phenomena of social life under universal principles or laws. Several of the examiners objected on the ground that there was nothing in Montesquieu that was not to be found in Aristotle—and so the examination was off to a good and indeed a traditional start. Durkheim employed all of his eloquence and his logic, refused to be intimidated by his examiners, and passed with high marks in spite of their ritual hostility.

A French translation of the Latin dissertation was published in 1937, and in 1953 it appeared together with another essay that Durkheim had written on Rousseau (*Montesquieu et Rousseau: Précurseurs de la sociologie*). Rousseau also was one of Durkheim's cultural heroes, so to speak, and a man he appreciated especially because of the clear emphasis on the importance of society in *The Social Contract*. Henri Peyre regards this essay as one of the most lucid ever written on Rousseau.

In 1893 Durkheim published, in Paris, his second dissertation, the famous *De la division du travail social: Étude sur l'organisation des sociétés supérieures,* to which we shall henceforth refer in its abbreviated English title as *The Division of Labor*. This is the first of the four principal works of Durkheim to which we shall give detailed attention in what follows. The year 1893 also produced some notes on the definition of socialism, a subject that was to occupy him two years later when he gave a course on the history of socialism at the University of Bordeaux. He had had an earlier interest in socialism and particularly in the relationship between individualism and socialism, but, beginning with his appointment at Bordeaux, he devoted his major efforts to the more definitely sociological works on which his fame was to rest. The lectures on socialism, however, are available now to the English reader in an edition translated by Charlotte Sattler and edited, with a superior introduction, by Alvin W. Gouldner in 1958.

Durkheim's second great book, *Les Règles de la méthode sociologique*, appeared in 1895, only two years after *The Division of Labor*. His third, *Le Suicide: Étude de sociologie,* appeared, again after a two-year interval, in 1897. Thus three of the most important works in the history of sociology appeared from the pen of one man in a period of only five years, 1893-1897. In 1898, as we have mentioned, Durkheim founded *L'-Année sociologique,* and during the following years he published four or five papers a year, and sometimes more, in this journal. *Les Formes élémentaires de la vie religieuse: Le système totémique en Australie,* some of which had also appeared as papers in the *Année* was published in 1912. These four books will be treated seriatim in the chapters that follow.

Many of the papers that poured from the prolific pen of Durkheim and appeared in his journal, and in other places as well, were later collected and published posthumously in book form. These include *Éducation et sociologie* (1922), *Sociologie et philosophie* (1924), *L'Éducation morale* (1925), *Le socialisme* (1928), *L'Évolution pédagogique en France* (1938), *Leçons de sociologie* (1950), *Montesquieu et Rousseau: Précurseurs de la sociologie* (1953), and *Pragmatisme et sociologie* (1955).

We have by no means seen the last of Durkheim's books. The second edition of Gouldner's *Socialism,* for example, appeared in 1962, and in 1963 Edward Sagarin translated, edited, and published Durkheim's long essay, "La Prohibition de l'inceste et ses origines," which appeared as the first article in the first volume of *L'Année sociologique*. In 1963 also, Rodney Needham translated and published, with a critical introduction, another long essay, entitled "Primitive Classification (De quelques formes primitives de classification: contribution à l'étude des représentations collectives), which Durkheim had written with Marcel Mauss and which first appeared in the sixth volume of *L'Année,* an even sixty years earlier.

There is no telling how many others will find it useful to reproduce, in one language or another, some of the papers of Durkheim. What is most needed is a definitive edition, in English, of all of his works. His importance, as we shall see, continues to grow as we move through years that are now more than a century removed from the date of his birth.

SELECTED

part 2 WORKS OF

DURKHEIM

I THE DIVISION OF LABOR

The Preface to the first edition of *The Division of Labor* establishes with clarity and emphasis the substantive purpose for which the book was written. The word "substantive" is used, of course, because the procedural purpose was to satisfy, in part, the requirements for the degree of Doctor of Philosophy at the École Normale Supérieure. The procedural detail has little significance in view of the startling and even dramatic statement with which Durkheim begins:

> This book is pre-eminently an attempt to treat the facts of the moral life according to the method of the positive sciences.*

What does it mean to treat the facts of the moral life as if they were susceptible to the rigorous yet rewarding requirements of the scientific method? It could mean something that Durkheim emphatically rejects. It could mean that propositions about morality are deducible from propositions about man and his activities that are to be found in the other sciences, and especially in biology and psychology. The notion that the nature of human activities, including those which are called "moral" or "immoral," can be deduced from principles discovered from the study of either the body or the mind is not one that appealed to Durkheim. Indeed, he was a lifelong opponent of such reductionism. Social facts, in-

*Émile Durkheim, *The Division of Labor in Society*, translated by George Simpson (Copyright 1933 by The Macmillan Company, New York; fourth printing 1960 by The Free Press of Glencoe, Illinois), p. 32.

cluding most especially moral facts, are phenomena of their own kind and can be studied and understood only in their own terms, in their own frame of reference, and on their own level.

In consequence, Durkheim introduces his first important book with the view that the moral life of man in society is a unique subject for investigation, that it is the prime responsibility of sociologists to undertake this investigation, and that a positive and scientific approach to this subject will contribute more to knowledge than any other approach could conceivably do.

At the same time Durkheim rejects any theory that would establish or assume an evolutionary connection between the moral facts of primitive societies and the moral facts of modern ones. He had little use for Spencer and was not a member of the evolutionary school of social interpretation that exercised so great—some would say so pernicious—an effect on social thought in England and the United States. "It is no longer possible to believe that moral evolution consists in the development of the same idea, confused and uncertain with primitive man, little by little growing clearer and more precise with the spontaneous progress of knowledge."* One cannot derive a contemporary morality, that is to say a sociological theory of modern morals, from a study of the Romans and their society, nor can one assume that what the Romans had in pristine form we now have in a more sophisticated form. Sociocultural conditions in Roman times were vastly different from those of modern times and no attempt to deduce the latter from the former, therefore, can hope to succeed. The evolutionary view is mistaken and must be rejected.

In both of these attitudes—the rejection of reductionism and the rejection of evolutionism—Durkheim cut himself off from two of the more promising of supports

*Ibid., p. 33.

for a science of sociology. It is true that he wrote long
before John B. Watson appeared on the scene with his
behaviorism, but stimulus-response psychology was in
the air, and Wundt, whose work he had known in Germany, and William James, whose *Principles of Psychology* appeared in 1890, were almost certainly in his consciousness as he explored the possibility of a kind of
knowledge called "sociology." The idea that the mo-
tions of the mind could be measured, to use a phrase as
old as Mencius, and that a scientific psychology might
supplant a "faculty" psychology, in which the psyche
had three faculties—the intellect, the emotions, and the
will—had clearly been advanced during the period of
Durkheim's graduate studies, and it was a notion that
might have tempted him as he sought the underpinnings
for a sociological theory. The point, however, is precisely this: sociology needs no underpinnings, it can
stand on its own feet, and it is a science *sui generis* because the principal object of its investigation—society
—is a phenomenon that is also *sui generis*.

A similar observation may be made about evolutionism. Here it is not psychology but history that becomes
dispensable for sociology. Durkheim rejects the autonomy and the inevitability of the historical process inso-
far as this process is presumed to provide an explanation for social facts. He did not believe that there are
necessary stages in the development of human societies
and that any given stage represents an evolutionary
emergent from the stage immediately preceding. So
prominent was the evolutionary doctrine in the last two
decades of the nineteenth century and so influential was
social Darwinism in England and the United States during this period that one tends to forget that it was not,
after all, a universal doctrine. At least one Frenchman
had other ideas, and it was these other ideas which went
into the making of his own kind of sociological inquiry.

There is yet another notion that Durkheim rejected
in the Preface to the first edition of his *Division of La-*

bor. This is that it is the primary business of sociology to "improve" society. No serious effort to acquire knowledge can be based upon so immediate and practical a design. The trouble with a goal of this kind is that it warps the judgment, substitutes short-range results for long-range contributions to knowledge, and makes science a handmaiden of politics rather than of philosophy. Durkheim's own words in this connection are important:

> Although we set out primarily to study reality, it does not follow that we do not wish to improve it; we should judge our researches to have no worth at all if they were to have only a speculative interest. If we separate carefully the theoretical from the practical problems, it is not to the neglect of the latter; but, on the contrary, to be in better position to solve them.*

This is a proposition that merits close and intelligent reflection. What does it mean?

It means that there is a difference between pure and applied science and that this difference may be ignored only to the detriment of both. The criterion of utility—whether personal or social—as a criterion of scientific significance can only, when it is not positively harmful, lead to delayed and confused applications of knowledge to the affairs of society. One of the most important of sociological laboratories, paradoxical as it might seem, is the ivory tower and no one who does not take up residence there for at least some time can hope to solve the problems of sociology, of science, or of society itself. It was Disraeli who remarked that it is the practical man who practices the blunders of his predecessors, and it was the late American philosopher, Morris Raphael Cohen, who said perhaps the finest word on this subject, something like the following: Purely theoretical

Ibid., p. 33.

contributions to mathematics and astronomy, by increasing the precision of navigation, have saved more lives at sea than any possible tinkering with the carpentry of lifeboats. The practical man, in short, wants to build a better lifeboat, and the goal is clearly a meritorious one. The theoretical man wants to study the stars, and on the surface his enterprise seems a useless one. Ultimately, however, the latter will save more lives than the former.

Science and social reform are two different kinds of activities. They can sometimes be performed by the same person, but it is an intellectual necessity to insist on the distinction between them. Science, including social science, can contribute to social reform and facilitate the tasks of reformers; but it is not itself reform nor should it be deluded by a criterion of immediate utility.

Still another question arises in Durkheim's Preface—whether there can be a scientific basis for ethics. It is an old question, and writers in different centuries and countries have given different answers to it. Durkheim answers in the affirmative. Although science can only foresee, but not command, it is nevertheless the case that science tells us what is necessary to life and, further, the supposition that man wishes to live, which Durkheim considers a simple proposition, "immediately transforms the laws science establishes into imperative rules of conduct." "To be sure," he continues, "it is then transformed into art; but the passage from science to art is made without a break. Even on the ultimate question, whether we ought to wish to live, we believe science is not silent."* There can, in short, be a science of ethics, and it is to this subject also that Durkheim intended his *Division of Labor* to make a contribution.

The following paragraph indicates without equivocation Durkheim's stand on this ancient issue:

*Ibid., p. 35.

Thus, the antithesis between science and ethics, that formidable argument with which the mystics of all times have wished to cloud human reason, disappears. To govern our relations with men, it is not necessary to resort to any other means than those which we use to govern our relations with things; thought, methodically employed, is sufficient in either case. What reconciles science and ethics is the science of ethics, for at the same time that it teaches us to respect the moral reality, it furnishes us the means to improve it.*

At the same time Durkheim wishes to conform to all of the canons of scientific method in his ethical inquiry—the use of "authentic proofs," the zeal for exactitude and precision, the careful observation of facts, and the treatment of facts in such a way that they will be objective and, if possible, measurable. Only in this way can the science of ethics conform to the high standards implied in its name.

The respect for facts does not entail the conclusion that all one does, in using the scientific method, is to gather more and more facts. Facts themselves, no matter how impressive the accumulation, do not of themselves constitute a science. "It is a vain delusion to believe that the best way to prepare for the advent of a science is first to accumulate patiently all the materials it will use, for one can know what these needed materials are only if there is already some presentiment of its essence and needs."† What Durkheim here calls a "presentiment" would be called in more contemporary terms an "hypothesis"—a notion, at the very least, of what questions the facts can answer. As John Dewey once remarked in a similar connection, facts are never given, they are always taken; and they are taken in terms of a conceptual scheme, in terms of some frame

*Ibid., p. 36.
†Ibid., p. 37.

of reference, in connection with some query that one wishes to address to them and expects—and hopes—that they will answer. Facts themselves can never constitute a science. If they could the telephone directory of the City of New York would be one.

These observations suggest that Durkheim had a sophisticated view of science and of the nature of its method. In the first place, as we have said, he regarded science as a method and not as a special kind of subject matter. Any subject, accordingly, including the moral life, can be approached scientifically. In the second place, he was alert to the dangers of reductionism so far as the social sciences, and particularly sociology, are concerned. In the third place, he saw—and advocated —the view that sociology possesses a unique subject matter and is unique in respect to substance but not with respect to method. In the fourth place, he recognized and emphasized the difference between the study of society and its reformation. The link between study and reform is a close one, and especially close when the study becomes scientific; but a distinction nevertheless remains. Closely related to it is the distinction between a pure and an applied science.

In all of these respects most American sociologists today would be in close agreement with Durkheim. Only his notion that there can be a science of ethics—as distinguished from a science of sociology—would invite dissent. It can be argued, perhaps, that there is too much ethics in sociology and not enough sociology in ethics, but even if this formulation should be cogent, it is not clear that sociology, as a positive science dealing in categorical propositions, could exhaust the nature of ethical inquiry, dealing as it does with normative ones. There is still an enormous difference between the determination of what is, on the one hand, and what ought to be, on the other. And here most contemporary sociologists would agree with Jeremy Bentham in saying that the word "ought" ought never to be used—except in saying it ought never to be used.

These preliminaries concluded, Durkheim addresses himself directly to his subject, the division of labor, and we shall accordingly follow in some detail the ideas he brings to it. Before doing so, however, we might suggest that the book as a whole is not an easy one, that Durkheim's thought is not as "formed" as it will be later on, and that he does not get to the meat of some of the important issues until he has spent some time on less important ones. Indeed, one has the impression throughout most of the book that Durkheim's writing is not really tight, that he uses a great many words in saying what he wants to say, and that some of these words are superfluous. The same observation may be made about the issues that Durkheim raises. Not all of them are relevant to his central theme. There is furthermore, in the writing, a certain, somewhat hesitant dogmatism of a kind that often characterizes the work of a young scholar. A "hesitant dogmatism," of course, is an oxymoron, an expression in which the adjective contradicts the noun it modifies. One has the impression that Durkheim indulges in overstatement at times, and with excessive emphasis, primarily because he lacks full confidence in the cogency of his arguments. In this respect *The Division of Labor* is a formative work, not a mature one.

All this, however, is incidental to what it is that Durkheim wants to say. He pronounces that the division of labor is one of the most basic of all of the phenomena of social life. Adam Smith had given currency to the expression itself, and when Durkheim wrote it had become the concern also of a number of other writers, including Schmoller, Simmel, and Bücher in Germany, and Maunier in France. The Industrial Revolution, with its factory system, had brought the matter to the forefront of consciousness in the intellectual world, and economists, publicists, and others were engaged in assessing both the narrowly economic and the more general social effects of specialization. What were its advantages and disadvantages? What were the various forms that it might take (sexual, regional, occupational, etc.)? In terms of what kind of unit can it be profitably discussed? These questions, and many others, appealed to the writers of the time.

Durkheim conceives his task to consist of three parts: first, to determine the function of the division of labor and to discover what social needs it satisfies; second, to seek its causes; and third, to inquire into what abnormalities and deviations, if any, it exhibits. In discussing the first of these Durkheim makes an important distinction between two different kinds of function. In the first sense the word "function" refers to any vital and continuous movement of parts and in this sense the word is almost synonymous with "activity." In the second, however, we have in mind also the consequence of the movement or the activity and in this sense we want to know also what needs are involved. In the first sense, in short, we mean by the function of something what it does; in the second what it satisfies. And it is in the second of these two senses that Durkheim intends to pursue his questions regarding the division of labor in society.

The problem that exists with respect to the division of labor is finding some connection between it and the moral life, which, it will be remembered, is the subject central to Durkheim's concerns and the one for the sake of which he examines all others. Although it is true, it is not enough to say that the division of labor is the source of civilization because the existence of civilization is not necessarily a moral fact. It may be in fact that civilization is devoid of moral implications. The notion that the division of labor may contribute to civilization, therefore, does not help us in the least because the morality is still missing. Some other solution to the problem must be found.

The solution, however, is not far away. It has often been asked whether social relations are motivated primarily by similarity or by dissimilarity, whether by likenesses or differences between people. Sociologists want to know which of the two is the sharper spur to interaction. Do we tend to associate with those who are most like us or with those in whom we discern an interesting difference? Aristotle, in the *Nicomachean Ethics,* addressed himself to this problem, especially as affecting the social relation of friendship, and Durkheim quotes him as follows:

> Friendship causes much discussion. According to some people, it consists in a certain resemblance, and we like those who resemble us: whence the proverbs "birds of a feather flock together" and "like seeks like," and other such phrases. Others, on the contrary, say that all who are alike are opposed to one another. . . . Heraclitus, again, maintains that "contrariety is expedient, and that the best agreement arises from things differing, and that all things come into being in the way of the principle of antagonism."*

Durkheim agrees that both similarity and dissimilarity are necessary to the development of "natural friendship," that difference as well as likeness can be involved in mutual attraction, and that, more specifically, it is certain kinds—not all kinds—of differences that attract one another. These considerations shed a new light on the division of labor; for it is the differentiation of duties and responsibilities that contributes to the solidarity of persons and that thus begins to take on a moral character. The conjugal relationship, for example, is an excellent illustration of this principle. The division of labor in the marital relationship cements the

*Aristotle, *Nicomachean Ethics,* VIII, 1, 1155a, 32.

union of the partners and it is therefore, so to speak, a moral cement. The sexual division of labor, in short, is one of the principal supports of conjugal solidarity. It is in this way that the division of labor rests at the very foundation of the social order.

Durkheim, incidentally, gives credit to Comte for having been the first to notice that the division of labor is not merely an economic phenomenon and that its ramifications extend far beyond the economic sphere. The subject itself is one to which only sociology—and neither economics nor psychology, nor both—can do full justice.

Durkheim is next ready to introduce some of the other considerations that, like the integrating character of the division of labor, have come to be associated with his name. He wants to know if there may be several types of social solidarity and he decides this question in the affirmative. There are, in fact, two types, one of which he calls "mechanical" solidarity and the other "organic" solidarity. He approaches this distinction through the law, where he observes that there are two types of punishments that are visited upon offenders—repressive sanctions and restitutive sanctions. The first of these consists of suffering or loss that is imposed upon the criminal and the second restores the *status quo*. The first is an actual punishment and the sum total of these sanctions make up the penal law. The second returns things to where they were and the sum total of these makes up civil, commercial, procedural, administrative, and constitutional law. To the first of these corresponds mechanical solidarity in society and to the second organic solidarity. The nature of crime and punishment thus helps to disclose the difference between two different kinds of social organization.

The difficulty of defining what it is to be a crime, of course, is one that Durkheim was not the first to confront—nor will he assuredly be the last. It is not necessary to pursue the problem as it appears to the moralist, the lawyer, or the criminologist. Durkheim arrives at his own definition by saying that "an act is criminal when it offends strong and defined states of the collective conscience," and it is this collective conscience which immediately engages our attention. "We must not say," Durkheim continues, "that an action shocks the common conscience because it is criminal, but rather that it is criminal because it shocks the common conscience. We do not reprove it because it is a crime, but it is a crime because we reprove it."*

What then is this common conscience, which easily established itself in the literature as one of Durkheim's most famous concepts? In the first place it is necessary to consider the original French expression, which is *la conscience collective*. The problem arises in knowing whether to translate *conscience* as "conscience" or as "consciousness," whether to give it a moral or a psychological connotation. Unfortunately, there is no good answer to this question, and for this reason it is best perhaps to leave it untranslated and to permit the text itself to determine in which of these two senses the word is being used. Durkheim defines it as the totality of beliefs and sentiments common to the average members of the same society, a totality that forms its own determinate system and has its own life. It has no specific organ or location but is diffused throughout an entire society. It maintains an independence of particular individuals, however, inasmuch as it precedes their appearance in society and survives their departure. It is common to all, of whatever geographic region and of whatever occupation. It is the link that unites one generation with another. Individuals move on through the stream of time, but the *conscience collective* endures. Although it is not something that individuals can themselves possess, it is both common to all of them and collective with respect to them. It is the totality of social

*Durkheim, *op. cit.*, p. 81.

similarities, the sentiments on which all persons in a given society agree. It is what is shocked by the commission of a crime and it is the *conscience collective,* in fact, that determines what it is to be a crime.

Perhaps the most interesting comment to be made about the *conscience collective* is that, in a large number of respects, it is similar to the concept of "culture" as it is used in modern social science. Culture, too, is independent of individuals, is something they share and hold in common, is something that moves through time from generation to generation (though not without change), and is synonymous with the social heritage. It is the unity of culture that defines a society. There are also, of course, certain differences between the *conscience collective* and culture. Durkheim gives to his concept a heavy moral emphasis, whereas morality is only one part—albeit an important part—of culture in its contemporary usage. Secondly, Durkheim's *conscience collective* does not include the material items and artifacts that the members of a society have, whereas the concept of culture often does so under the label of "material culture." Unfortunately, there is no standardized definition of "culture" in contemporary sociology and the customs of different writers in their use of it would conform sometimes more and sometimes less closely with Durkheim's own connotation.

The important consideration, however, is not the minor similarities or differences in connotation between the two concepts but the remarkable fact that they both perform the same basic function. They help to give to society a reality of its own, an autonomy, a certifiable independence of the individuals who make it up. One might say that they give stuff and substance to society. Only the sociologically unsophisticated would think that society is exhausted by the individuals who comprise it. It is individuals, on the contrary, who receive stature, significance, and indeed personality by holding in common a *conscience collective,* by sharing a culture. With the help of these concepts one can understand the nature of society as something objective, as something *there,* and not merely as a name for a collection of individuals, a collection, moreover, that would vanish if the individuals in it were simply enumerated. This is one of Durkheim's greatest contributions and he introduces it almost incidentally as a phenomenon that explains the nature and definition of crime and punishment.

This part of the Durkheimian doctrine, however, received a poor reception in many places, not least the United States. Whether one translated it as "collective conscience" or "collective consciousness," the *conscience collective* looked too much like a group mind to win acceptance in a pragmatic, particularistic, individualistic society. It is true that there is a certain metaphysical extravagance in Durkheim's language, and it is quite correct to insist that groups do not have minds or consciences or consciousness, and that only people—not groups or societies—can think democratic thoughts, eat apple pie, hit home runs, paint their fingernails, and practice monogamy. Nevertheless, there must be something that enables us to characterize American society, for example, as pragmatic, particularistic, and individualistic—and this is what Durkheim was trying to explain. It was altogether too hasty to dismiss Durkheim's concept, and sometimes the author himself, on the ground that he had confused an abstraction with reality. Society needs something like a *conscience collective* to give it definition, but the language gives too many hostages to an indefensible metaphysics. The concept of culture, on the contrary, does everything that the *conscience collective* was designed to do, and it does it without metaphysical overtones.

In pursuing the problem of punishment Durkheim adumbrates a position that he will explore later on in *The Elementary Forms of the Religious Life.* He maintains that penal law is essentially religious in origin and that religion itself is essentially a social phenomenon.

Those who might be inclined to suggest that religion exists for the individual and can be used by him for the pursuit or satisfaction of personal ends are almost certainly wrong. Religion, like society itself, is external to the individual and exerts a certain constraint upon him. The sacrifices it requires him to make, whether small or large, are not altogether pleasant. He makes them anyway. The criminal law in a primitive society is religious law, and the interests it serves are social. The degree to which religion is a social rather than a supernatural phenomenon will be elaborated at some length later on, but it is of some significance to see a hint of what is to come in the earliest of Durkheim's books.

In his chapter on mechanical solidarity, Durkheim expresses another principle that, though not original with him, has found its way into the textbooks of sociology and that, indeed, is a matter of common observation. Sometimes it is discussed as a simple function of the in-group–out-group distinction. It concerns the cohesion that a group of people can experience when they are threatened, as a group, from the outside. No matter what discord may obtain among them, they tend to unite in the face of a common enemy. It is when we are abroad that we appreciate our compatriots the most, and even seek them out; and similarly it is when our religion is subjected to intolerance or discrimination or persecution that we are most highly aware of what we have in common with our colleagues or co-religionists. "Of course, we always love the company of those who feel and think as we do, but it is with passion, and no longer solely with pleasure, that we seek it immediately after discussions where our common beliefs have been greatly combated."*

The commission of a crime has the same effect. The people gather to gossip and to shake their heads; an affront to the common conscience has been committed;

Ibid., p. 102.

their solidarity is increased. Crime damages the *conscience collective* and it is the *conscience collective* that resists. The offense is against the community and not merely against the victim. Here again we can see the meaning and the significance of the *conscience collective*. We see also the type of solidarity, namely mechanical solidarity, that the penal law exists to maintain.

Durkheim seems to take a kind of pride in the paradoxical conclusion to which his reasoning leads him. It leads him to assert that, far over and above the effect punishment might have on those who commit crimes, it has another and more important function, and that is to heal the wounds of the law-abiding, the wounds caused by assault upon their common sentiments. Punishment thus serves the community and contributes to the integration of society.

Organic solidarity is a phenomenon of a different kind. The law that appears in it is no longer a law of punishment but rather a law of restitution. Its function is not to expiate but rather to restore. The disturbance that gives rise to it is not interpreted as an assault upon community sentiment nor does it involve the *conscience collective*. We can sometimes be quite indifferent to the outcome of litigation and observe it without passion or excitement. Further, whereas repressive law remains diffuse throughout the community, restitutive law has its special organs and institutions—tribunals, councils, functionaries, and so on.

Nevertheless, the operation of restitutive law is not merely a matter of the conciliation or reconciliation of private interests. If it were, it would have nothing to do with solidarity. Even when contracts are made between individuals, it is society that gives them their sanctity and guarantees their enforcement. The operation of restitutive law is in fact the application of general rules to particular cases, and it is the general rules above all that grow out of the use and wont of society. Even when restitutive sanctions, as Durkheim says, are

strangers to the *conscience collective,* society is not
wholly absent. If contracts have the power to bind, it is
society that is the source of this power, and furthermore
it is a power that can be invoked only when the contracts conform to the general rules of law and, what is
more, have something of a moral value. Thus, in the
United States today the instrument of the law may not
be invoked to support a housing covenant that contains
exclusion clauses on the ground of race or that otherwise permits a racial or religious discrimination.

Durkheim views contracts as a form of legal recognition of the existence of the division of labor. A contract
imposes different duties and obligations upon the con-
tracting parties; they enter into it for the sake of cooperation; and cooperation in turn is participation in a
common pursuit. If the tasks to be undertaken are of
the same kind, then we have a simple division of labor;
if they are qualitatively different, then we have a compound division of labor, or specialization proper. It is
the latter, of course, that is most often governed by contract. Contractual relations often become quite complicated, and this in turn testifies to the extent of the division of labor in modern societies.

Durkheim is thus prepared to summarize the
differences between mechanical and organic solidarity.
In the first, an individual is bound to society without
any intermediary; in the second, he is dependent upon
the parts of which society is composed. Society itself
means something different in these two instances—in
the first it is a totality of beliefs and sentiments, a *conscience collective;* in the second it is a system of interre-
lated and interdependent functions, a system, in short,
that exhibits a division of labor. The first is the solidarity of similarity, the second the solidarity of difference.
The first Durkheim calls "mechanical" only because the
parts, like the molecules of inorganic bodies, have no
actions of their own; the individual conscience depends
upon the collective conscience, and participates in such

actions as the latter makes; the individual is in a sense absorbed into the collective personality. The second he calls "organic" because it produces the kind of integration we see in the higher animals, where each organ has its own specialized function.

The differences between mechanical and organic solidarity are clear. A comparable distinction, with different labels, can be found in the work of almost every sociologist, Durkheim's predecessors and successors alike. Durkheim does more than make the distinction, however, when he suggests that it is the latter, the organic solidarity, that contributes more than the former to social cohesion. As labor is divided, so also does each member of society depend more and more upon his neighbor. The labor of one fits into the labor of the other and produces a cohesive community. Even as the community is more cohesive and better integrated, however, so at the same time does the individual become more free, more able to exercise his initiative, less tightly bound by common sentiment. The division thus contributes both to the cohesion of society and to the self-expression and freedom of the individual. This is the essence of the Durkheimian thesis.

Enthusiasm for his thesis leads Durkheim astray at certain points. One of these points is quaint enough to amuse and may be briefly mentioned. Durkheim offered as further proof of his thesis the notion that the more primitive a society is the more indistinguishable its members become, the one from the other; thus, one aboriginal American resembles every other aboriginal American. Among more advanced peoples, on the contrary, one can easily distinguish one individual from another. What is (erroneously) affecting Durkheim here, of course, is another facet of the in-group—out-group principle; namely, that we tend to categorize and to stereotype those who are in the out-group, who thereupon seem to us to be only members of a class; whereas we react to those in our in-groups as individuals and thus perceive the differences between them. Durkheim even thought that Frenchmen of his day resembled one another less than they did at an earlier time, and that it was the increasing division of labor that contributed to the heterogeneity of appearances among them.

The notion that societies become more heterogeneous as they move through time is a Spencerian one. It was Herbert Spencer who adopted and propounded the extreme form of this doctrine and who concocted a famous—and almost unreadable—definition of evolution as follows: "Evolution is an integration of matter and concomitant dissipation of motion; during which the matter passes from an indefinite, incoherent homogeneity to a definite, coherent heterogeneity; and during which the retained motion undergoes a parallel transformation." (William James, incidentally, once "translated" this definition into "Evolution is a change from a no-howish untalkaboutable all-alikeness to a somehowish and in general talkaboutable not-all-alikeness by continuous sticktogetherations and somethingelsifications.") There is no question of the fact that Spencer exerted an influence on Durkheim, as the many references to the English sociologist in *The Division of Labor* will testify, but Durkheim had patently less enthusiasm for the doctrine of evolution in general than he had for the notion of increasing heterogeneity. Indeed, he specifically disclaimed the view that the different social types are stages in an ascending linear series.

Much of the remainder of Durkheim's book is devoted to strengthening the argument that the *conscience collective* is extensive and strong in the more primitive societies and becomes weaker as the division of labor increases. There is an increasing gain of organic solidarity over mechanical solidarity and this process Durkheim again illustrates with reference to the development of the law. One of his arguments merits a moment of attention, and that is that, when solidarity is weak, it is easy for immigrants to be introduced, accepted, and assimilated into a society. Durkheim offers a number of examples of this, ranging from ancient Rome, where citizenship was easily acquired, to the Indians of North America, where even captives could become members of the tribe after appropriate ceremony. These processes become much more difficult, however, in societies with an advanced division of labor because in them the integration is of a different kind. In general, mechanical solidarity links members of a society together much less strongly than organic solidarity and it is the latter that is increasingly in evidence over the course of time.

This, then, assumes for Durkheim the stature of a sociological law; namely, that the linkages and ties that stem from similarity, and therefore from the *conscience collective,* progressively slacken and give way to stronger ties that are consequences of the division of labor. Durkheim's own words are worth repeating:

> This law, in itself, is already enough to show the tremendous grandeur of the role of the division of labor. In sum, since mechanical solidarity progressively becomes enfeebled, life properly social must decrease or another solidarity must slowly come in to take the place of that which has gone. The choice must be made. In vain shall we contend that the collective conscience extends and grows stronger at the same time as that of individuals. We have just proved that the two terms vary in a sense inverse to each other. Social progress, however, does not consist in a continual dissolution. On the contrary, the more we advance, the more profoundly do societies reveal the sentiment of self and of unity. There must, then, be some other social link which produces this result; this cannot be any other than the division of labor.

If, moreover, one recalls that even where it is most resistant, mechanical solidarity does not link men with the same force as the division of labor, and that, moreover, it leaves outside its scope the major part of phenomena actually social, it will become still more evident that social solidarity tends to become exclusively organic. It is the division of labor which, more and more, fills the role that was formerly filled by the common conscience. It is the principal bond of social aggregates of higher types.*

This is the reason that the division of labor is so very much more important than the economists assumed. It is in fact one of the basic processes in society. Mechanical solidarity gives way to organic solidarity, and at the same time the *conscience collective,* which explains the unity and integration of the more primitive society, relinquishes its unifying function to the division of labor.

It should be said that Durkheim never forgets the moral component that belongs to these processes. Altruism, for example, is not merely an agreeable ornament of social life but one of its very necessities. Men cannot live together, Durkheim says, without acknowledging their need for one another, and this need of course increases with a developing division of labor. Every society is a moral society, but it is the advanced society, the one that has a division of labor, that makes clear to every member of it how much he depends upon other members and how true it is that it is from society that he receives everything that he needs. This recognition helps to form his sentiments and gives to his cooperation a moral character.

If one grants the cogency of Durkheim's general theory regarding the division of labor, it then becomes necessary to follow him a little in his discussion of how it is that this division comes about. To what is it due? How does it happen? What are its causes? One consideration that has no relevance, incidentally, is that the

Ibid., p. 173.

division of labor occurs because it increases our happiness. If this were the case, civilization would have stopped long ago, because there are definite limits to our happiness and because happiness itself is associated with a golden mean and not with the continuous increase in this or that quality. To do one's duty, for example, is a moral virtue, but all duty is limited. It is limited by other duties. There can be excesses of morality, which contribute in turn to the deterioration of morality. In any event, no one would seriously contend that happiness increases with the advancement of man and his societies.

The reasons for this disquisition on happiness are not altogether clear. When it is concluded, however, Durkheim addresses himself again to the causes of the division of labor. He finds a primary cause in the material and moral density of society. By "material density" he means simply "population density" and the degree to which the population is dispersed or concentrated in a given society. The growth of cities is clear evidence, of course, of an increase in material density. Increasing concentration of population, however, brings with it an increasingly intense interaction among people, and new ways of communication and transportation decrease the vacant spaces among the various segments of a society. This is density of a different kind. Durkheim calls it "moral density"—and he uses it sometimes synonymously with the concept of "social volume." Societies become more "voluminous" as they advance and there is a consequent increase in the division of labor.

Durkheim is thus ready to formulate another law as follows: "The division of labor varies in direct ratio with the volume and density of societies, and, if it progresses in a continuous manner in the course of social development, it is because societies become regularly denser and generally more voluminous."*

*Ibid., p. 262.

It is important to realize that the increasing density not only permits an increase in the division of labor; it necessitates it. Density is thus the determining cause. The struggle for existence also plays a part—and in this respect Durkheim speaks in consciously Darwinian tones —but it is a struggle that has softened, so to speak, and has become sublimated in other processes. The division of labor cannot be conceived either as an expression or as a consequence of conflict.

Before bringing his book to a close, Durkheim examines a number of so-called secondary factors that are also involved in the division of labor, including, for example, heredity, a factor that has more force for Durkheim than it has for anyone today. It is fair to say, however, that for him too heredity loses its hold as civilization advances, and indeed he offers several cogent arguments for this conclusion. On this subject Durkheim's treatment is quite modern when measured by the time in which he wrote, a time antedating all of the arguments about the relative importance of heredity and environment that were to plague the social sciences for at least a decade and half in the twentieth century.

The division of labor, finally, is synonymous with civilization itself, and, in finding the causes of the former, we have also explained the latter. Civilization is a necessary consequence of changes in the volume and density of societies; it is a phenomenon that must happen, not because men desire it but because it is an inevitable accompaniment of the increasing intensity of their interactions.

Except for three brief chapters on abnormal forms of the division of labor, two of which are called the "anomic" and the "forced," these observations on civilization bring Durkheim's book to its conclusion. In what follows we shall reprint two excerpts. The first of these is the section in which he discusses the point made immediately above, namely, the relationship between the division of labor and civilization. The second is his own

conclusion, in which he summarizes the results of his
effort in this work and gives a final emphasis to his
theme.

The Collective Conscience*

The totality of beliefs and sentiments common to average citizens of the same society forms a determinate
system which has its own life; one may call it the *collective* or *common conscience*. No doubt, it has not a
specific organ as a substratum; it is, by definition,
diffuse in every reach of society. Nevertheless, it has
specific characteristics which make it a distinct reality.
It is, in effect, independent of the particular conditions
in which individuals are placed; they pass on and it remains. It is the same in the North and in the South, in
great cities and in small, in different professions.
Moreover, it does not change with each generation, but,
on the contrary, it connects successive generations with
one another. It is, thus, an entirely different thing from
particular consciences, although it can be realized only
through them. It is the psychical type of society, a type
which has its properties, its conditions of existence, its
mode of development, just as individual types, although
in a different way. Thus understood, it has the right to
be denoted by a special word. The one which we have
just employed is not, it is true, without ambiguity. As
the terms, collective and social, are often considered
synonymous, one is inclined to believe that the collective conscience is the total social conscience, that is, to
extend it to include more than the psychic life of society,
although, particularly in advanced societies, it is only a
very restricted part. Judicial, governmental, scientific,

*Émile Durkheim, *op. cit.,* pp. 79–85.

industrial, in short, all special functions are of a psychic nature, since they consist in systems of representations and actions. They, however, are surely outside the common conscience. To avoid the confusion into which some have fallen, the best way would be to create a technical expression especially to designate the totality of social similitudes. However, since the use of a new word, when not absolutely necessary, is not without inconvenience, we shall employ the well-worn expression, collective or common conscience, but we shall always mean the strict sense in which we have taken it.

We can, then, to resume the preceding analysis, say that an act is criminal when it offends strong and defined states of the collective conscience.

The statement of this proposition is not generally called into question, but it is ordinarily given a sense very different from that which it ought to convey. We take it as if it expressed, not the essential property of crime, but one of its repercussions. We well know that crime violates very pervasive and intense sentiments, but we believe that this pervasiveness and this intensity derive from the criminal character of the act, which consequently remains to be defined. We do not deny that every delict is universally reproved, but we take as agreed that the reprobation to which it is subjected results from its delictness. But we are hard put to say what this delictness consists of. In immorality which is particularly serious? I wish such were the case, but that is to reply to the question by putting one word in place of another, for it is precisely the problem to understand what this immorality is, and especially this particular immorality which society reproves by means of organized punishment and which constitutes criminality. It can evidently come only from one or several characteristics common to all criminological types. The only one which would satisfy this condition is that opposition between a crime, whatever it is, and certain collective sentiments. It is, accordingly, this opposition which makes crime rather than being a derivative of crime. In other words, we must not say that an action shocks the common conscience because it is criminal, but rather that it is criminal because it shocks the common conscience. We do not reprove it because it is a crime, but it is a crime because we reprove it. As for the intrinsic nature of these sentiments, it is impossible to specify them. They have the most diverse objects and cannot be encompassed in a single formula. We can say that they relate neither to vital interests of society nor to a minimum of justice. All these definitions are inadequate. By this alone can we recognize it: a sentiment, whatever its origin and end, is found in all consciences with a certain degree of force and precision, and every action which violates it is a crime. Contemporary psychology is more and more reverting to the idea of Spinoza, according to which things are good because we like them, as against our liking them because they are good. What is primary is the tendency, the inclination; the pleasure and pain are only derivative facts. It is just so in social life. An act is socially bad because society disproves of it. But, it will be asked, are there not some collective sentiments which result from pleasure and pain which society feels from contact with their ends? No doubt, but they do not all have this origin. A great many, if not the larger part, come from other causes. Everything that leads activity to assume a definite form can give rise to habits, whence result tendencies which must be satisfied. Moreover, it is these latter tendencies which alone are truly fundamental. The others are only special forms and more determinate. Thus, to find charm in such and such an object, collective sensibility must already be constituted so as to be able to enjoy it. If the corresponding sentiments are abolished, the most harmful act to society will not only be tolerated, but even honored and proposed as an example. Pleasure is incapable of creating an impulse out of whole cloth; it can only link those sentiments which exist to such and such a particular end, provided that the end be in accord with their original nature.

There are, however, some cases where the preceding does not explain. There are some actions which are more severely repressed than they are strongly reproved by general opinion. Thus, a coalition of functionaries, the encroachment of judicial authority on administrative authority, religious functions on civil functions, are the object of a repression which is not in accord with the indignation that they arouse in consciences. The appropriation of public goods leaves us quite indifferent, and yet is punished quite severely. It may even happen that the act punished may not directly hurt any collective sentiment. There is nothing in us which protests against fishing and hunting out of season, or against overloaded conveyances on the public highway. But there is no reason for separating these delicts from others; every radical distinction would be arbitrary, since they all present, in different degree, the same external criterion. No doubt, in any of these examples, the punishment does not appear unjust. But if it is not enforced by public opinion, such opinion, left to itself, would either not object to it at all, or show itself less insistent. Thus, in all cases of this type, delictness does not come about, or does not entirely derive from the vivacity of the collective sentiments which are offended, but comes from some other cause.

It is surely true that once a governmental power is instituted, it has, by itself, enough force to attach a penal sanction spontaneously to certain rules of conduct. It is capable, by its own action, of creating certain delicts or of increasing the criminological value of certain others. So, all the actions that we have just cited present this common character of being directed against some administrative organ of social life. Must we then admit that there are two kinds of crimes coming from two different causes? Such an hypothesis cannot be considered. As numerous as the varieties are, crime is everywhere essentially the same, since it everywhere calls forth the same effect, in respect of punishment, which, if it can be more or less intense, does not by that change its nature. But the same fact cannot have two causes, unless this duality is only apparent, and basically they are one. The power of reaction which is proper to the State ought, then, to be of the same sort as that which is diffused throughout society.

And where would it come from? From the depth of the interests which the State cares for and which demand protection in a very special way? But we know that the subversion of even deep interests does not alone suffice to determine the penal reaction; it must still be felt in a very decided way. How does it come about that the least damage done to a governmental organ is punished, although many much more severe disorders in other social organs are reparable only civilly? The smallest injury to the police power calls forth a penalty, while even repeated violation of contracts, or constant lack of correctness in economic relations only asks amends for the loss. Doubtless, the system of direction plays an eminent role in social life, but there are others whose interest is of great importance, yet whose functioning is not assured in this fashion. If the brain have its importance, the stomach is an organ which is likewise essential, and the sicknesses of one are menaces to life just as those of the other. Why is this privilege accorded to what is sometimes called the social brain?

The difficulty resolves itself easily if we notice that, wherever a directive power is established, its primary and principal function is to create respect for the beliefs, traditions, and collective practices; that is, to defend the common conscience against all enemies within and without. It thus becomes its symbol, its living expression in the eyes of all. Thus, the life which is in the collective conscience is communicated to the directive organ as the affinities of ideas are communicated to the words which represent them, and that is how it assumes a character which puts it above all others. It is no longer a more or less important social function; it is the collective type incarnate. It participates in the authority which the latter exercises over consciences, and it is from there that it draws its force. Once constituted, however, without freeing itself from the source whence it flows and whence it continues to draw its sustenance, it nevertheless becomes an autonomous factor in social life, capable of spontaneously producing its own movements without external impulsion, precisely because of the supremacy which it has acquired. Since, moreover, it is only a derivation from the force which is immanent in the collective conscience, it necessarily has the same properties and reacts in the same manner, although the latter does not react completely in unison. It repulses every antagonistic force as would the diffuse soul of society, although the latter does not feel this antagonism, or rather, does not feel it so directly. That is, it considers as criminal, actions which shock it without, however, shocking the collective sentiments in the same degree. But it is from these latter that it receives all the power which permits it to create crimes and delicts. Besides, not coming from without or arising from nothing, the following facts, which will be amply developed in the rest of this work, confirm this explanation. The extent of the activity which the governmental organ exercises over the number and the qualification of criminal acts depends on the force it receives. That can be measured either by the extent of the authority which it exercises over citizens, or by the degree of gravity recognized in crimes directed against it. But we shall see that it is in lower societies that this authority is greatest and this gravity most elevated, and moreover, that it is in these same social types that the collective conscience has the most power.

Thus, we must always return to this last; that is whence, directly or indirectly, comes all criminality.

Crime is not simply the disruption even of serious interests; it is an offense against an authority in some way transcendent. But, from experience, there is no moral force superior to the individual save collective force.

Conclusion*

I   We are now in a position to solve the practical problem that we posed for ourselves at the beginning of this work.

If there is one rule of conduct which is incontestable, it is that which orders us to realize in ourselves the essential traits of the collective type. Among lower peoples, this reaches its greatest rigor. There, one's first duty is to resemble everybody else, not to have anything personal about one's beliefs or actions. In more advanced societies, required likenesses are less numerous; the absence of some likenesses, however, is still a sign of moral failure. Of course, crime falls into fewer different categories; but today, as heretofore, if a criminal is the object of reprobation, it is because he is unlike us. Likewise, in lesser degree, acts simply immoral and prohibited as such are those which evince dissemblances less profound but nevertheless considered serious. Is this not the case with the rule which common morality expresses when it orders a man to be a man in every sense of the word, which is to say, to have all the ideas and sentiments which go to make up a human conscience? No doubt, if this formula is taken literally, the man prescribed would be man in general and not one of some particular social species. But, in reality, this human conscience that we must integrally realize is nothing else than the collective conscience of the group

*Ibid., pp. 396–409.

of which we are a part. For what can it be composed of, if not the ideas and sentiments to which we are most attached? Where can we find the traits of our model, if not within us and around us? If we believe that this collective ideal is that of all humanity, that is because it has become so abstract and general that it appears fitting for all men indiscriminately. But, really, every people makes for itself some particular conception of this type which pertains to its personal temperament. Each represents it in its own image. Even the moralist who thinks he can, through thought, overcome the influence of transient ideas, cannot do so, for he is impregnated with them, and no matter what he does, he finds these precepts in the body of his deductions. That is why each nation has its own school of moral philosophy conforming to its character.

On the other hand, we have shown that this rule has as its function the prevention of all agitation of the common conscience, and, consequently, of social solidarity, and that it could accomplish this role only by having a moral character. It is impossible for offenses against the most fundamental collective sentiments to be tolerated without the disintegration of society, and it is necessary to combat them with the aid of the particularly energetic reaction which attaches to moral rules.

But the contrary rule, which orders us to specialize, has exactly the same function. It also is necessary for the cohesion of societies, at least at a certain period in their evolution. Of course, its solidarity is different from the preceding, but though it is different, it is no less indispensable. Higher societies can maintain themselves in equilibrium only if labor is divided; the attraction of like for like less and less suffices to produce this result. If, then, the moral character of the first of these rules is necessary to the playing of its role, it is no less necessary to the second. They both correspond to the same social need, but satisfy the need differently, because the conditions of existence in the societies themselves differ.

Consequently, without speculating concerning the first principle of ethics, we can induce the moral value of one from the moral value of the other. If, from certain points of view, there is a real antagonism between them, that is not because they serve different ends. On the contrary, it is because they lead to the same end, but through opposed means. Accordingly, there is no necessity for choosing between them once for all nor of condemning one in the name of the other. What is necessary is to give each, at each moment in history, the place that is fitting to it.

Perhaps we can even generalize further in this matter.

The requirements of our subject have obliged us to classify moral rules and to review the principal types. We are thus in a better position than we were in the beginning to see, or at least to conjecture, not only upon the external sign, but also upon the internal character which is common to all of them and which can serve to define them. We have put them into two groups: rules with repressive sanctions, which may be diffuse or organized, and rules with restitutive sanctions. We have seen that the first of these express the conditions of the solidarity, *sui generis,* which comes from resemblances, and to which we have given the name mechanical; the second, the conditions of negative solidarity and organic solidarity. We can thus say that, in general, the characteristic of moral rules is that they enunciate the fundamental conditions of social solidarity. Law and morality are the totality of ties which bind each of us to society, which make a unitary, coherent aggregate of the mass of individuals. Everything which is a source of solidarity is moral, everything which forces man to take account of other men is moral, everything which forces him to regulate his conduct through something other than the striving of his ego is moral, and morality is as solid as these ties are numerous and strong. We can see how inexact it is to define it, as is often done, through liberty. It rather consists in a state of dependence. Far from serving to emancipate the individual, or disengaging him from the environment which surrounds him, it has, on the contrary, the function of making him an integral part of a whole, and, consequently, of depriving him of some liberty of movement. We sometimes, it is true, come across people not without nobility who find the idea of such dependence intolerable. But that is because they do not perceive the source from which their own morality flows, since these sources are very deep. Conscience is a bad judge of what goes on in the depths of a person, because it does not penetrate to them.

Society is not, then, as has often been thought, a stranger to the moral world, or something which has only secondary repercussions upon it. It is, on the contrary, the necessary condition of its existence. It is not a simple juxtaposition of individuals who bring an intrinsic morality with them, but rather man is a moral being only because he lives in society, since morality consists in being solidary with a group and varying with his solidarity. Let all social life disappear, and moral life will disappear with it, since it would no longer have any objective. The state of nature of the philosophers of the eighteenth century, if not immoral, is, at least, *amoral*. Rousseau himself recognized this. Through this, however, we do not come upon the formula which expresses morality as a function of social interest. To be sure, society cannot exist if its parts are not solidary, but solidarity is only one of its conditions of existence. There are many others which are no less necessary and which are not moral. Moreover, it can happen that, in the system of ties which make up morality, there are some which are not useful in themselves or which have power without any relation to their degree of utility. The idea of utility does not enter as an essential element in our definition.

As for what is called individual morality, if we understand by that a totality of duties of which the individual would, at the same time, be subject and object, and which would link him only to himself, and which would, consequently, exist even if he were solitary,— that is an abstract conception which has no relation to reality. Morality, in all its forms, is never met with except in society. It never varies except in relation to social conditions. To ask what it would be if societies did not exist is thus to depart from facts and enter the domain of gratuitous hypotheses and unverifiable flights of the imagination. The duties of the individual towards himself are, in reality, duties towards society. They correspond to certain collective sentiments which he cannot offend, whether the offended and the offender are one and the same person, or whether they are distinct. Today, for example, there is in all healthy consciences a very lively sense of respect for human dignity, to which we are supposed to conform as much in our relations with ourselves as in our relations with others, and this constitutes the essential quality of what is called individual morality. Every act which contravenes this is censured, even when the agent and the sufferer are the same person. That is why, according to the Kantian formula, we ought to respect human personality wherever we find it, which is to say, in ourselves as in those like us. The sentiment of which it is the object is not less offended in one case than in the other.

But not only does the division of labor present the character by which we have defined morality; it more and more tends to become the essential condition of social solidarity. As we advance in the evolutionary scale, the ties which bind the individual to his family, to his native soil, to traditions which the past has given to him, to collective group usages, become loose. More mobile, he changes his environment more easily, leaves his people to go elsewhere to live a more autonomous existence, to a greater extent forms his own ideas and sentiments. Of course, the whole common conscience does not, on this account, pass out of existence. At least there will always remain this cult of personality, of individual dignity of which we have just been speaking, and which, today, is the rallying-point of so many people. But how little a thing it is when one contemplates the ever increasing extent of social life, and, consequently, of individual consciences! For, as they become more voluminous, as intelligence becomes richer, activity more varied, in order for morality to remain attached to the group with a force equal to that of yesterday, the ties which bind him to it must become stronger and more numerous. If, then, he formed no others than those which come from resemblances, the effacement of the segmental type would be accompanied by a systematic debasement of morality. Man would no longer be sufficiently obligated; he would no longer feel about and above him this salutary pressure of society which moderates his egoism and makes him a moral being. This is what gives moral value to the division of labor. Through it, the individual becomes cognizant of his dependence upon society; from it come the forces which keep him in check and restrain him. In short, since the division of labor becomes the chief source of social solidarity, it becomes, at the same time, the foundation of the moral order.

We can then say that, in higher societies, our duty is not to spread our activity over a large surface, but to concentrate and specialize it. We must contract our horizon, choose a definite task and immerse ourselves in it completely, instead of trying to make ourselves a sort of creative masterpiece, quite complete, which contains its worth in itself and not in the services that it renders. Finally, this specialization ought to be pushed as far as the elevation of the social type, without assigning any other limit to it. No doubt, we ought so to work as to realize in ourselves the collective type as it exists. There are common sentiments, common ideas, without which, as has been said, one is not a man. The rule which orders us to specialize remains limited by the contrary rule. Our conclusion is not that it is good to press specialization as far as possible, but as far as necessary. As for the part that is to be played by these two opposing necessities, that is determined by experience and cannot be calculated *a priori*. It is enough for us to have shown that the second is not of a different nature from the first, but that it also is moral, and that, moreover, this duty becomes ever more important and pressing, because the general qualities which are in question suffice less and less to socialize the individual.

It is not without reason that public sentiment reproves an ever more pronounced tendency on the part of dilettantes and even others to be taken up with an exclusively general culture and refuse to take any part in occupational organization. That is because they are not sufficiently attached to society, or, if one wishes, society is not sufficiently attached to them, and they escape it. Precisely because they feel its effect neither with vivacity nor with the continuity that is necessary, they have no cognizance of all the obligations their positions as social beings demand of them. The general ideal to which they are attached being, for the reasons we have spoken of, formal and shifting, it cannot take them out of themselves. We do not cling to very much when we have no very determined objective, and consequently, we cannot very well elevate ourselves beyond a more or less refined egotism. On the contrary, he who gives himself over to a definite task is, at every moment, struck by the sentiment of common solidarity in the thousand duties of occupational morality.

II But does not the division of labor by making each of us an incomplete being bring on a diminution of individual personality? That is a reproach which has often been levelled at it.

Let us first of all remark that it is difficult to see why

it would be more in keeping with the logic of human nature to develop superficially rather than profoundly. Why would a more extensive activity, but more dispersed, be superior to a more concentrated, but circumscribed, activity? Why would there be more dignity in being complete and mediocre, rather than in living a more specialized, but more intense life, particularly if it is thus possible for us to find what we have lost in this specialization, through our association with other beings who have what we lack and who complete us? We take off from the principle that man ought to realize his nature as man, to accomplish his *olkelov epyov,* as Aristotle said. But this nature does not remain constant throughout history; it is modified with societies. Among lower peoples, the proper duty of man is to resemble his companions, to realize in himself all the traits of the collective type which are then confounded, much more than today, with the human type. But, in more advanced societies, his nature is, in large part, to be an organ of society, and his proper duty, consequently, is to play his role as an organ.

Moreover, far from being trammelled by the progress of specialization, individual personality develops with the division of labor.

To be a person is to be an autonomous source of action. Man acquires this quality only in so far as there is something in him which is his alone and which individualizes him, as he is something more than a simple incarnation of the generic type of his race and his group. It will be said that he is endowed with free will and that is enough to establish his personality. But although there may be some of this liberty in him, an object of so many discussions, it is not this metaphysical, impersonal invariable attribute which can serve as the unique basis for concrete personality, which is empirical and variable with individuals. That could not be constituted by the wholly abstract power of choice between two opposites, but it is still necessary for this faculty to be exercised towards ends and aims which are proper to the agent. In other words, the very materials of conscience must have a personal character. But we have seen in the second book of this work that this result is progressively produced as the division of labor progresses. The effacement of the segmental type, at the same time that it necessitates a very great specialization, partially lifts the individual conscience from the organic environment which supports it, as from the social environment which envelops it, and, accordingly, because of this double emancipation, the individual becomes more of an independent factor in his own conduct. The division of labor itself contributes to this enfranchisement, for individual natures, while specializing, become more complex, and by that are in part freed from collective action and hereditary influences which can only enforce themselves upon simple, general things.

It is, accordingly, a real illusion which makes us believe that personality was so much more complete when the division of labor had penetrated less. No doubt, in looking from without at the diversity of occupations which the individual then embraces, it may seem that he is developing in a very free and complete manner. But, in reality, this activity which he manifests is not really his. It is society, it is the race acting in and through him; he is only the intermediary through which they realize themselves. His liberty is only apparent and his personality borrowed. Because the life of these societies is, in certain respects, less regular, we imagine that original talents have more opportunity for free play, that it is easier for each one to pursue his own tastes, that a very large place is left to free fantasy. But this is to forget that personal sentiments are then very rare. If the motives which govern conduct do not appear as periodically as they do today, they do not leave off being collective, and, consequently, impersonal, and it is the same with the actions that they inspire. Moreover, we have shown above how activity becomes richer and more intense as it becomes more specialized.

Thus, the progress of individual personality and that of the division of labor depend upon one and the same cause. It is thus impossible to desire one without desiring the other. But no one today contests the obligatory character of the rule which orders us to be more and more of a person.

One last consideration will make us see to what extent the division of labor is linked with our whole moral life.

Men have long dreamt of finally realizing in fact the ideal of human fraternity. People pray for a state where war will no longer be the law of international relations, where relations between societies will be pacifically regulated, as those between individuals already are, where all men will collaborate in the same work and live the same life. Although these aspirations are in part neutralized by those which have as their object the particular society of which we are a part, they have not left off being active and are even gaining in force. But they can be satisfied only if all men form one society, subject to the same laws. For, just as private conflicts can be regulated only by the action of the society in which the individuals live, so intersocial conflicts can be regulated only by a society which comprises in its scope all others. The only power which can serve to moderate individual egotism is the power of the group; the only power which can serve to moderate the egotism of groups is that of some other group which embraces them.

Truly, when the problem has been posed in these terms, we must recognize that this ideal is not on the verge of being integrally realized, for there are too many intellectual and moral diversities between different social types existing together on the earth to admit of fraternalization in the same society. But what is possible is that societies of the same type may come together, and it is, indeed, in this direction that evolution appears to move. We have already seen that among European peoples there is a tendency to form, by spontaneous movement, a European society which has, at present, some idea of itself and the beginning of organization. If the formation of a single human society is forever impossible, a fact which has not been proved, at least the formation of continually larger societies brings us vaguely near the goal. These facts, moreover, in no wise contradict the definition of morality that we have given, for if we cling to humanity and if we ought to cling to it, it is because it is a society which is in process of realizing itself in this way, and with which we are solidary.

But we know that greater societies cannot be formed except through the development of the division of labor, for not only could they not maintain themselves in equilibrium without a greater specialization of functions, but even the increase in the number of those competing would suffice to produce this result mechanically; and that, so much the more, since the growth of volume is generally accompanied by a growth in density. We can then formulate the following proposition: the ideal of human fraternity can be realized only in proportion to the progress of the division of labor. We must choose: either to renounce our dream, if we refuse further to circumscribe our activity, or else to push forward its accomplishment under the condition we have just set forth.

III But if the division of labor produces solidarity, it is not only because it makes each individual an *exchangist,* as the economists say; it is because it creates among men an entire system of rights and duties which link them together in a durable way. Just as social similitudes give rise to a law and a morality which protect

them, so the division of labor gives rise to rules which
assure pacific and regular concourse of divided functions. If economists have believed that it would bring
forth an abiding solidarity, in some manner of its own
making, and if, accordingly, they have held that human
societies could and would resolve themselves into purely economic associations, that is because they believed
that it affected only individual, temporary interests.
Consequently, to estimate the interests in conflict and
the way in which they ought to equilibrate, that is to
say, to determine the conditions under which exchange
ought to take place, is solely a matter of individual
competence; and, since these interests are in a perpetual
state of becoming, there is no place for any permanent
regulation. But such a conception is, in all ways, inadequate for the facts. The division of labor does not present individuals to one another, but social functions.
And society is interested in the play of the latter; in so
far as they regularly concur, or do not concur, it will be
healthy or ill. Its existence thus depends upon them,
and the more they are divided the greater its dependence. That is why it cannot leave them in a state of in-
determination. In addition to this, they are determined
by themselves. Thus are formed those rules whose number grows as labor is divided, and whose absence makes
organic solidarity either impossible or imperfect.

But it is not enough that there be rules; they must be
just, and for that it is necessary for the external conditions of competition to be equal. If, moreover, we remember that the collective conscience is becoming
more and more a cult of the individual, we shall see
that what characterizes the morality of organized societies, compared to that of segmental societies, is that
there is something more human, therefore more rational, about them. It does not direct our activities to ends
which do not immediately concern us; it does not make
us servants of ideal powers of a nature other than our

own, which follow their directions without occupying themselves with the interests of men. It only asks that we be thoughtful of our fellows and that we be just, that we fulfill our duty, that we work at the function we can best execute, and receive the just reward for our services. The rules which constitute it do not have a constraining force which snuffs out free thought; but, because they are rather made for us and, in a certain sense, by us, we are free. We wish to understand them; we do not fear to change them. We must, however, guard against finding such an ideal inadequate on the pretext that it is too earthly and too much to our liking. An ideal is not more elevated because more transcendent, but because it leads us to vaster perspectives. What is important is not that it tower high above us, until it becomes a stranger to our lives, but that it open to our activity a large enough field. This is far from being on the verge of realization. We know only too well what a laborious work it is to erect this society where each individual will have the place he merits, will be rewarded as he deserves, where everybody, accordingly, will spontaneously work for the good of all and of each. Indeed, a moral code is not above another because it commands in a drier and more authoritarian manner, or because it is more sheltered from reflection. Of course, it must attach us to something besides ourselves but it is not necessary for it to chain us to it with impregnable bonds.

It has been said with justice that morality—and by that must be understood, not only moral doctrines, but customs—is going through a real crisis. What precedes can help us to understand the nature and causes of this sick condition. Profound changes have been produced in the structure of our societies in a very short time; they have been freed from the segmental type with a rapidity and in proportions such as have never before been seen in history. Accordingly, the morality which corresponds to this social type has regressed, but without another developing quickly enough to fill the ground that the first left vacant in our consciences. Our faith has been troubled; tradition has lost its sway; individual judgment has been freed from collective judgment. But, on the other hand, the functions which have been disrupted in the course of the upheaval have not had the time to adjust themselves to one another; the new life which has emerged so suddenly has not been able to be completely organized, and above all, it has not been organized in a way to satisfy the need for justice which has grown more ardent in our hearts. If this be so, the remedy for the evil is not to seek to resuscitate traditions and practices which, no longer responding to present conditions of society, can only live an artificial, false existence. What we must do to relieve this anomy is to discover the means for making the organs which are still wasting themselves in discordant movements harmoniously concur by introducing into their relations more justice by more and more extenuating the external inequalities which are the source of the evil. Our illness is not, then, as has often been believed, of an intellectual sort; it has more profound causes. We shall not suffer because we no longer know on what theoretical notion to base the morality we have been practicing, but because, in certain of its parts, this morality is irremediably shattered, and that which is necessary to us is only in process of formation. Our anxiety does not arise because the criticism of scholars has broken down the traditional explanation we used to give to our duties; consequently, it is not a new philosophical system which will relieve the situation. Because certain of our duties are no longer founded in the reality of things, a breakdown has resulted which will be repaired only in so far as a new discipline is established and consolidated. In short, our first duty is to make a moral code for ourselves. Such a work cannot be improvised in the silence of the study; it can arise only through itself, little by little, under the pressure of internal causes which make it necessary. But the service that thought can and must render is in fixing the goal that we must attain. That is what we have tried to do.

II THE RULES OF SOCIOLOGICAL METHOD

The Rules of Sociological Method, which Durkheim published in 1895, is quite simply one of the classics of social science. In it Durkheim continues the tradition of Auguste Comte in insisting that sociology is—or at the very least ought to be—a science, a science moreover that conforms to all of the canons of evidence that the physical sciences exhibit and subjects itself to all of the same rules of verification. In order for sociology to arrive at this superior state it is necessary to know something about the methods of science and to show how these methods can also be utilized in the study of social phenomena. This is the task to which Durkheim devotes himself in this book.

Durkheim's intent is never clearer than it is in the first words of his Preface to the first edition:

We are so little accustomed to treat social phenomena scientifically that certain of the propositions contained in this book may well surprise the reader. However, if there is to be a social science, we shall expect it not merely to paraphrase the traditional prejudices of the common man but to give us a new and different view of them; for the aim of all science is to make discoveries, and every discovery more or less disturbs accepted ideas. Unless, then, sociology attributes to common sense an authority which it has not enjoyed for a long time in other sciences—and it is impossible to see how such authority could be justified—the scholar must resolutely resist being intimidated by the results to which his researches lead, demanding only that they be conducted scientifically.

As it is characteristic of the sophist to invite paradoxes, likewise it is a sign of intellectual cowardliness to avoid them when they are imposed on us by the facts.*

Science begins, one might say, with the mistrust of common sense, and this is almost especially the case with sociology because it is sociology that deals with things ordinarily taken for granted by common sense. It should not be necessary to insist, for example, that we live in societies, that all men everywhere have lived in societies, and that these societies exhibit certain regularities, and even uniformities. Society in short has a structure and it is the business of sociology to disclose it. Societies also change, and this becomes the second of the problems that require study. All this knowledge would seem to be derivable from commonsense observation.

This, nevertheless, is a proposition that Durkheim and all other sociologists deny. Common sense can never be a reliable guide to a scientific conclusion. The trouble with common sense is that it is sense that is common only to certain varieties and kinds of people— those who inhabit the same cave that we do, to invoke both the Platonic and the Baconian figure. Durkheim is well aware of this when he remarks on how difficult the impulses of common sense are to eradicate from our consciousness, especially in sociological discussion, and how deeply ingrained, and how, even when we are aware of them, they continue to afflict our unconscious judgments. We must all recognize that the ways of thinking to which we are most inclined are apt to be harmful rather than beneficial in the scientific study of society.

In this Preface, Durkheim also gives himself a label

*Émile Durkheim, *The Rules of Sociological Method,* translated by S. A. Solovay and J. H. Mueller, and edited by G. E. G. Catlin (New York: The Free Press of Glencoe, 1962, eighth edition), p. xxxvii.

—that of rationalist. For a Frenchman to call himself a rationalist, of course, should occasion no surprise. All Frenchmen are rationalists. They have been rationalists at least since Descartes and they are rationalists still. But it is significant that Durkheim should have made a point of it and significant for us too to recognize that by the scientific study of society he means a rational study and not necessarily, or not only, an empirical one. He has faith, as he says, in the future of reason.

Sociology, like the other sciences, is concerned with facts, not speculations, and the problem therefore becomes one of defining what it is to be a social fact. This problem is the first one to engage Durkheim's attention in the text proper. In every society there are phenomena that differ from those which attract the attention of physical scientists. We pay our bills in a certain way, honor our contracts, use currency, conform to customs, obey the law, participate in religious life, and follow a profession—and all of these activities have their origin and locus outside the consciousness of the individual. They are ways of doing things that antedate the appearance of any individual in his own society and will doubtless endure after his disappearance. They are unplanned and undetermined by the individual. The individual, on the contrary, has to learn them and conform to them. They are in every sense external to him, and it is this exteriority that is Durkheim's first criterion of a social fact.

There is a second criterion. Social facts are not only exterior; they are also coercive. If we fail to obey the law, something happens to us. If we violate a contract, something else happens to us. If we refuse to follow the patterns of our profession, we shall put our success in jeopardy. If we indulge in forms of dress that differ too much from those of our associates, we invite their ridicule. And if we violate the morals or shock the beliefs held by our contemporaries to be sacred, we shall suffer the consequences of ostracism. Some of these sanctions, to be sure, may be indirectly rather than directly applied. No one will seem to care if I follow practices in my business that are medieval rather than modern, and indeed they will not care. But there will be consequences sooner or later and they will induce me to care. Similarly, there is no law that requires the use of the French language and none that requires the use of the legal currency of France, and consequently no legal punishment for abstention from both of these practices. It is difficult to see, nevertheless, how a Frenchman could get along without either of them. These, then, are the two characteristics of social facts—exteriority and constraint.

These facts, now, are highly distinctive. They are clearly not biological and they are just as clearly not psychological. They exist neither in the body nor in the individual consciousness. Their locus is in society; they are social facts; and it is only to them that the adjective "social" should be applied. They constitute the proper domain of sociology and give to this science its unique character. Sociology then deals with a limited range of phenomena, but these phenomena are exclusively social and are not shared by any of the other sciences. This is clarion language and is meant to subdue the doubts of those who, in Durkheim's time, expressed some scepticism about the very existence of sociology, who maintained either that there was no separate category of facts that such a science could call its own or that, if there were such a category, it could not be approached with the objective and rational methods of science. This first chapter, entitled "What Is a Social Fact?", is so suggestive and so important that we reproduce it in its entirety in this book.

How then do we study social facts? The first rule is to consider them as *things*. Up to the present time—i.e., Durkheim's time—sociology had unfortunately concerned itself with concepts rather than things. Comte had made a brave effort to consider social phenomena

as natural objects, but he too was soon caught up in the
filaments of theory, where facts succumb to ideas.
Furthermore, he lapsed from objectivity when he began
to believe in an increasing perfection of human nature
and in the progress of humanity. Humanity is not itself
a social fact; it does not exist at all. The only facts we
can observe are the facts of development of the separate societies, some past and some more recent, some in
one part of the world and some in another. Science
knows nothing of humanity.

Spencer's sociology has similar faults. Spencer had
made a distinction between so-called military societies
on the one hand and industrial societies on the other.
The difference is in the kind of cooperation that obtains
in them. In the former, cooperation is directed toward a
common end; in the latter to private ends. There are
some affinities here to Durkheim's differentiation
between mechanical and organic solidarity. Durkheim
does not, however, seem to recognize the point that
Spencer was making because his own mention of military and industrial societies occurs in quite a different
context. Durkheim is here concerned to show only that
Spencer had abandoned facts for ideas and had thus diminished the sociological significance of his work. Durkheim wants facts, not ideas, and neither his mentor,
Comte, nor the famous Englishman, was able to meet
his own high standards in this respect. Spencer may
claim to be among those who proceed empirically but
actually he was much more interested in arguments
than he was in facts, and in theories rather than things.

These same unfortunate tendencies, that is, the substitution of ideas for facts, can be observed also in ethics, which Durkheim of course regarded as a branch of
sociology, and in political economy. In this respect
Durkheim indulges in some rather severe strictures
about economics and especially the economics of John
Stuart Mill. His conclusion is that both ethics and economics are seriously deficient in their use of scientific

methods and that both of these inquiries belong in fact to the arts rather than to the sciences. Psychology, too, was once in this unfortunate position, but recent developments have effected transformations in it, changing it from a subjective discipline to an objective science. The same remains to be done for sociology.

Durkheim believed that this transformation would be easier to accomplish in sociology than it was in psychology. Psychology, dealing as it does with states of mind, has the problem of getting outside, as it were, and of viewing mental phenomena from an external vantage point. This it is enormously difficult to do. Social facts, on the contrary, are external by definition and therefore there is little reason that they cannot be treated initially as objective. They clearly have this advantage over psychological facts, that they qualify initially and immediately as things; by their intrinsic nature they stand outside the consciousness of individuals. Law, for example, is objectified in written codes, the currents of daily life in statistics, fashions in costumes, and taste in works of art. From this point of view one might predict that sociology will overtake psychology in its movement to become an objective science. Even though social facts may be more complex than psychic facts, the sociologist has the advantage that he can follow a path cut first by the psychologist.

A rigorous discipline, however, is needed in order to find the way through the subjective wilderness and emerge on the other side onto the cultivated soil of science. It is necessary to observe carefully certain rules of which the first is to eradicate all preconceptions. This in essence is necessary in all the sciences, in our day as it was at the time of Descartes. Indeed, it was Descartes who first insisted on this procedure as essential to the pursuit of truth. Bacon had something similar in mind when he discussed his famous "idols," those biases and prejudices which creep into our inquiries and impair their objectivity. It is equally necessary for the sociologist to emancipate himself from all those ideas which may afflict him as a member of society, as one of this group or that, and to consider them in their pristine dress, or nakedness, as the case may be. Of course, as Durkheim is willing to admit, it is not easy to dispel sentiment and emotion from our sociological research. We are members of society after all—we are even patriots—and are thus susceptible to all the currents of opinion that surround us. One even has to accept the scorn that is bound to be directed against anyone who tries, for example, to study morality objectively, the scorn contained in Wordsworth's contumely—although Durkheim does not use this example—for the philosopher, "a fingering slave, one that would peep and botanize on his mother's grave." All of these things one must do in order to earn and to deserve the name of sociologist.

If eradication of preconceptions, the first rule of method, is a negative kind of statement, a proscription rather than a prescription, the second rule on the contrary is a positive one. This second rule is the old Aristotelian recommendation to define the terms with which one is going to operate. Durkheim's language in fact takes on an Aristotelian color when he deals with definition and particularly when he says that definitions must deal with phenomena "in terms of their inherent properties" and "elements essential to their nature." The Aristotelian notion of fixed essences, and of essence and accident, no longer prevails in the philosophy of science, but the modifications in it were made after Durkheim's time. In any event Durkheim formulates his second rule as follows: "The subject matter of every sociological study should comprise a group of phenomena defined in advance by certain common external characteristics, and all phenomena so defined should be included within this group."* The rule of definition is

*Ibid., p. 35.

particularly important in sociology because most of the time we are dealing with words—family, property, crime—that already have meanings in ordinary speech, and the ambiguous connotations they have there may interfere with the precision of scientific communication. Attention to these simple rules, for example, will save us from the error of assuming that savages have no morality when the truth of the matter is that they conform in all respects to a morality of their own, different from ours but binding upon them.

There is a third rule that the sociologist must observe. Although our definitions proceed, and properly so, from our perceptions of things, we must nevertheless be on guard lest these perceptions, like sensations in general, distort the object we are investigating. The objectivity that one of our sense perceptions may have is directly related to the stability of the object perceived and thus we have to care about the establishment of constant points of reference. The sociologist has to learn to separate the idiosyncrasies of individual perceptions from the more stable substratum of the objects themselves, and thus Durkheim formulates his third rule as follows: "When, then, the sociologist undertakes the investigation of some order of social facts, he must endeavor to consider them from an aspect that is independent of their individual manifestations."* Observance of this rule, more practically speaking, will permit us to distinguish the peculiarities of family systems reported by travelers, missionaries, and explorers from the underlying reality of family forms.

There are additional rules for separating the pathological from the normal in human societies. In introducing this subject, Durkheim reverts to the ancient and perhaps somewhat tiresome problem—discussed also in *The Division of Labor*—of whether science, in addition to telling us what is, can tell us also what ought to

Ibid., p. 45.

be. Can there, in short, be a scientific basis for ethics or do ethical decisions forever escape the domain of facts? To this question there are obviously two answers, an affirmative, offered by those who believe in the possibility of a science of ethics, and a negative, offered by those who do not. Among recent philosophers, for example, we find John Dewey and Bertrand Russell on opposite sides. Dewey devoted a good part of his writings to a most sophisticated effort to derive ethical principles from scientific postulates or, better, from scientific procedures, whereas Russell contended that normative judgments (i.e., those which contain the word "ought") are not only outside the realm of science; they are equally far outside the realm of knowledge. Russell's position agrees with that of an unnamed writer quoted by Durkheim to the effect that science can indeed illuminate the world, but it leaves our hearts in darkness.

Durkheim believes, however, that once it is granted that health is better than disease, it is possible for science to discover in all sorts of phenomena the difference between their normal and their pathological manifestations, and one has thereupon a chance to choose the former rather than the latter on the basis of the scientific discrimination between them. In this realm, however, empirical proof is difficult and one has to rely therefore on rational arguments. The case is easier with respect to individuals than with respect to societies. One knows from the mortality statistics, for example, that rheumatic disease is dangerous to health. One has no similar kind of evidence for the health or sickness of the social organism. It is nevertheless possible to make a discrimination in terms of the degree of diffusion of certain phenomena and to call normal those which are widely distributed, in all or most individuals, and abnormal or pathological those which are not. Durkheim seems to be sure that the social phenomena that are most widespread, whether forms of organization or anything else, are in the aggregate the most advantageous, and that greater frequency is itself an index of superiority. He offers however no arguments for this thesis, except what appears to him to be its reasonableness, and one can only say that the contemporary reader would have some difficulty in accepting it on that ground. Durkheim does recognize, however, that a form may still be universal long after it has lost its utility. In that case the sociologist confronts the problem of determining the original cause of the phenomenon and an investigation into whether or not it continues to operate in its original fashion.

Since this point is a little confusing—and perhaps Durkheim was not himself so clear on it as he might have been—it may be well to quote a few of his comments:

> After having established by observation that a particular fact is general, he [the sociologist] will go back to the conditions which determined this generality in the past and will then investigate whether these conditions are still given in the present or if, on the contrary, they have changed. In the first case he may properly designate the phenomenon as normal; and, in the second, refuse it this designation. For example, in order to determine whether the present economic state of Europe, with the absence of organization characterizing it, is normal or not, we shall investigate the causes which brought it about. If these conditions still exist in our present-day society, this situation is normal in spite of the dissent it arouses. But if, on the contrary, it is found to be related to the old social structure which we have elsewhere qualified as segmental and which, after having been the essential framework of societies, progressively disappears, we shall have to conclude that the present situation, however universal, is pathological.

By the same method should be settled all controversial questions of this kind, such as those concerning the normality of the decline in religious beliefs or of the development of state powers.*

Durkheim is certainly too sanguine—almost to the point of naiveté—in his belief that great issues of public policy such as the ones he mentions can be decided scientifically on the basis of any such determination of "normality," especially when normality is associated with universality or general diffusion. The only possible explanation for his involvement in this problem is his desire to give some practical and moral importance to sociology. His solution of it, however, is less than satisfactory. The argument from diffusion and universality leads him to the conclusion that crime is a normal social phenomenon, even if the criminal is an abnormal individual. What is more curious, however, is that he accepts this conclusion with delight as a paradox that was at one time puzzling even to himself, and permits himself a final word in which he maintains that crime is not only normal, it is also necessary and useful because the conditions of which it is a part "are themselves indispensable to the normal evolution of morality and law."†

When Durkheim finishes this rather unsatisfactory chapter, a chapter that leaves the distasteful impression of the "good boy" expressing perverse sentiments solely on the basis of his superior ability to defend them, he turns to something of greater sociological significance— namely, the problem of the classification of social types. The problem that motivates him is one that penetrates to the very center of a social science. There are two contrary approaches to the nature of collective life. One of these, favored by the historians, maintains what

*Ibid., pp. 61–62.
†Ibid., p. 70.

might be called a "nominalistic" position (in the medieval sense) and asserts that every society is different to the point of being unique and that therefore generalizations are impossible. The second, favored by the philosophers, maintains what might be called a "realistic" position (also in the medieval sense) and asserts on the contrary that there is only one humanity and that what is true for one grouping of people—whether tribe, city-state, or nation—is true for all, and consequently that one can deduce the characteristics of human societies from generalizations about the nature of human nature. Due almost without doubt to the realization that the first of these positions would make sociology impossible and that the second would make it unnecessary, Durkheim endeavors to find a middle ground. This he does with his notion of the social type, or social species. In this latter view, we find both the diversity that the facts display and the unity that scientific principles require. It is true that the institutions of society exhibit endless variations, but these variations, on the other hand, are susceptible to scientific treatment at a level of abstraction that makes them all members of a class.

How, then, does one arrive at a social species, how does one substitute a limited number of classes or types for an infinite variety of individuals? The question, as can be seen, has rather large implications for sociology. It has frequently been said that in some respects we are like all other people, in other respects like some other people, and in still other respects like no one except ourselves. It is clear that, in the first of these respects, we are particularly the concern of such general sciences as physiology, neurology, and psychology. In the last, we are subjects for biography. It is in the second, the respect that we are like some other people and different from some others that we become the proper objects for sociological inquiry. It is in this framework that Durkheim attempts to offer his views of the nature of a social species.

The problem, then, is one of "social morphology." One way to solve it is to begin, as Spencer did, with simple aggregates and to follow them with more complex types, still considered as combinations of the aggregates. The trouble arises when we endeavor to say what is simple and what is complex. It is by no means certain that the societies we call "primitive" were as simple as they have seemed and it is not at all clear that they did not exhibit certain complexities of their own. It is only after criticizing Spencer's view, however, that Durkheim seems to adopt it, and to find in the primitive horde something simple enough to serve as a basis for the classification of social species. Using as a definition of a simple society one that does not include within itself any more simple aggregate, Durkheim finds the horde to be "the protoplasm of the social realm, and, consequently, the natural basis of classification."

From this beginning the classification is built up to include clan, tribe, phratry, curia, confederation, city-state, and empire—although the details are left incomplete. Here Durkheim is interested more in example than in comprehensiveness of treatment. Actually, as he says, it is not only the number and nature of component elements that constitute a social species but also its mode of composition. One can have a species, incidentally, even if it has only one member, like, for example, the Roman Empire. One may not, however, classify societies by their state or degree of civilization because the result of this procedure would be not social species but rather historical phases. This, in effect, is Durkheim's criticism of Comte and of some of the evolutionists as well.

When Durkheim turns his attention to the problem of the explanation of social facts, he says several things that merit a modicum of comment. One of them is that social facts are not always useful to the societies in which they appear. Just as organ is sometimes independent of function in biology—i.e., just as the same organ can sometimes serve entirely different ends—so social facts in society can sometimes serve one purpose and sometimes an entirely different one. We can also observe the phenomenon of the persistence of facts after their utility has disappeared. Just as old words may express new ideas, so old social forms, like judicial oaths, religious dogmas, and laws, can remain after their original function has changed. This is the phenomenon that we today call a "cultural survival," and Durkheim's description of it is both clear and discriminating.

Because the same social form may fulfill different social functions, it is necessary, in our sociological inquiry, to distinguish between the function it fulfills and the efficient cause that produces it. Durkheim prefers the word "function" to "end" or "purpose" both because social phenomena do not necessarily exist for the useful results they produce and because end and purpose imply intent, which is too subjective for treatment. Durkheim is not wholly hostile to teleological explanations, but regards them as belonging rather more properly to philosophy than to sociology. The dismissal of teleology, however, does not mean that we are required to overlook the effects of social facts. Indeed, cause and effect are correlative phenomena, each depends upon the other, and both are necessary for the complete explanation of a phenomenon. "Consequently," in conclusion of this point, "to explain a social fact it is not enough to show the cause on which it depends; we must also, at least in most cases, show its function in the establishment of social order."* Any attempt to utilize teleological modes of explanation has the unfortunate effect of making sociology disappear in favor of psychology, and this, of course, is anathema to Durkheim. "If society is only a system of means instituted by men to attain certain ends, these ends can only be individ-

Ibid., p. 97.

ual,"* and consequently it is only from the individual
that the needs and desires that determine the existence
of societies could have come. Society therefore can be
explained only in terms of the individual, and in individual consciousness is to be found the source of all social evolution. On this reading, sociological laws would
only be corollaries of psychological laws and the ultimate explanation of society would be furnished by psychology. In Durkheim's view both Comte and Spencer
were guilty of adopting this erroneous procedure, as
were several other sociologists of a lesser stature. Indeed, family organization is often explained by the sentiments parents have for children and children for parents, marriage by the conveniences it confers upon both
partners, punishment by anger, economic life by the
desire for wealth, morality by the duty that the individual feels, and religion by the wonder and fear that the
forces of nature awaken in him.

Needless to say, this view Durkheim regards as wholly fallacious. Such an interpretation of social phenomena would result in a radical alteration of their fundamental nature. Since their basic characteristic is the
ability to exert constraint upon individual consciousness, they cannot possibly be derived from individual consciousness and sociology cannot therefore be
a corollary of psychology. Durkheim warms to his
theme:

> For this power of constraint is evidence of the fact
> that social phenomena possess a different nature
> from ours, since they control us only by force or, at
> the very least, by weighing upon us more or less
> heavily. If social life were merely an extension of the
> individual being, it would not thus ascend toward its
> source, namely, the individual, and impetuously in-
> vade it. If the authority before which the individual
> bows when he acts, feels, or thinks socially governs

*Ibid., p. 97.

him to this extent, it does so because it is a product of social forces which transcend him and for which he, consequently, cannot account. The external impulse to which he submits cannot come from him, nor can it be explained by what happens within him.*

We have got to explain social life by social facts and not social life by psychological facts. Society surpasses the individual both in time and in space and it accounts for him rather than he for it. Society imposes upon the individual ways of thinking, of feeling, and of acting that "it has consecrated with its prestige," and this pressure is the distinctive property of social facts.

It is wholly erroneous, furthermore, to consider society as merely a sum of individuals. Individuals are necessary, of course, in order for society to exist but they are not sufficient for its explanation. Social facts are not individual facts, sociological phenomena are not psychological phenomena, and the collective conscience is not an individual conscience. It is Durkheim's firmness on this last point in fact that tends to cause trouble if *conscience* is translated "consciousness" rather than "conscience," because then it comes to be feared that he is conferring reality upon a collective consciousness and thus creating a group mind. This brings in its train the metaphysical difficulties mentioned in the preceding chapter. This is one of the reasons, as we have remarked before, that Durkheim received so indifferent a reception in American sociology. If his metaphysics is questionable, however, his emphasis is unmistakable. In one famous sentence he goes so far as to insist that "every time that a social phenomenon is directly explained by a psychological phenomenon, we may be sure that the explanation is false."† This sentence, one feels, de-

Ibid., p. 101.
†*Ibid.,* p. 104.

serves an exclamation point instead of the period with which it ends. Though less familiar, another statement deserves a similar fame; namely, that the source of all that is obligatory is outside the individual. If one reflects upon the meaning of this assertion, one becomes conscious of its weight and significance. The section in which these opinions appear is so important that we reproduce it in this book.

The saliency of these views can be recognized not only in the stable and organized groups that permeate a society but also in those temporary and evanescent groupings we call "crowds." Even there, and possibly even especially there, the constraints are so great, and so great are the pressures operating upon the individual, that he is apt to indulge in sentiments and activities that are foreign to those he would express in other circumstances. They may in fact be quite opposed to them, and this once again exhibits the power and the dominance of society. How much more must this be the case when the influences stem from an organized rather than an unorganized group, when the pressures, so to speak, are institutionalized and constant rather than haphazard and intermittent.

Actually, this conclusion does not necessarily follow; that is, the pressures to conform when one is a member of a crowd—and even more a mob—are probably greater, at least in the short run, than when one is a member of a highly organized group, say a church or a corporation. But the pressures are there in any event, and clearly Durkheim did not have the comparative point in mind. And once again, in this connection, he indulges in an impressive statement in opposition to psychology: "A purely psychological explanation of social facts cannot fail, therefore, to allow all that is characteristic (i.e., social) in them to escape."*

*Ibid., p. 106.

The reason for the inability of psychology to explain social phenomena is in fact quite clear and easy to comprehend. It is simply this—and sociologists as disparate as Durkheim and Weber (in the *Protestant Ethic*) have both mentioned it—that it is impossible to explain a variable by a constant. Psychological factors are simply too constant in their effects to be able to explain the particular variations that characterize social institutions. Although they may prompt the appearance of certain manifestations, they do not call forth any one social form in preference to another and cannot therefore explain any of them. Finally, no one has ever been able to discover any inner spring of human nature or of human character that could explain the course of social evolution. In psychological terms, at least, this evolution must remain a mystery. One is perfectly free, of course, to postulate some innate human tendency toward progress, but to speak in this way is to indulge in psychological aberrations rather than in sociological facts.

These considerations lead to the formulation of a sociological law, namely, "The determining cause of a social fact should be sought among the social facts preceding it and not among the states of the individual consciousness."* Durkheim italicizes this law, perhaps unnecessarily. It is consonant with his entire philosophy of sociology and, in fact, is one of its necessary corollaries. Similarly, for the sake of completion, and again italicized, "The function of a social fact ought always to be sought in its relation to some social end."† Both of these principles appear again and again in sociological literature, most notably perhaps in the long—and famous—methodological note to *The Polish Peasant in Europe and America,* by William I. Thomas and Florian

Ibid., p. 110.
†*Ibid.*, pp. 110–11.

Znaniecki, a book that has been called the one sure classic of American sociology.

In a passage toward the end of *The Rules of Sociological Method,* Durkheim returns to a subject that engaged his attention in *The Division of Labor,* namely, the basic reason for the latter phenomenon. It will be remembered that he found this reason in population density—not a crude material density of people as such, but rather a dynamic density involving the quantity and kind of social interaction. Almost as if he had neglected to give a full explanation in his earlier volume, he now defines dynamic density as a function of the number of individuals who are having *social*—as distinguished from purely commercial—relations with one another, as the degree of fusion in the social segments, and as the degree of participation in social life. Here he corrects what he regards as a careless statement in his earlier work and makes much wider the separation between the material density that corresponds to purely economic interaction on the one hand and the dynamic density that defines the broader sphere of social interaction. Density, in short, is to be conceived of neither as a demographic nor as an economic but rather as a social phenomenon.

In the last of his chapters in this book, Durkheim draws a distinction between the experimental method, in which the investigator can actually manipulate the variables, and the comparative method, in which he is limited to observation. Since experimentation is obviously impossible for the most part where society is concerned, the sociologist is fairly well limited to the latter, the comparative method. Comte, it is true, attempted a historical method in addition, but Durkheim does not ascribe much importance to this on the ground that for scientific purposes it is necessary to detach social phenomena from particular chronological sequences. His arguments here open up an entirely new range of problems, and it cannot be said that he treated them in the detail that they warrant. Durkheim also, as before, indulges in a number of strictures upon John Stuart Mill, and particularly the method of "residues," which he regards as inappropriate in the investigation of social phenomena. Of the other canons of induction to which Mill gave classic expression, Durkheim clearly prefers concomitant variation to either the method of agreement or the method of difference; indeed he regards concomitant variation as the method par excellence of sociological research. This is particularly the case because of the brevity of the inventories that sociologists are able to take into account in their study of total societies. As soon as one discovers that two phenomena vary together, it is not necessary to observe a large number of cases in order to suspect the presence of a sociological law.

In its application of the comparative method, sociology finally has the possibility of utilizing facts from a single society, from several societies of the same species, and of different societies altogether, thus widening considerably the range of data. One cannot explain a social fact of any complexity without considering it in the widest possible social context and by following its development in all kinds of societies. The comparative method is thus not a particular branch of sociology; it is sociology itself to the degree that it ceases to be purely descriptive and endeavors to explain repetition and regularity. In order to give validity to these comparisons, however, it is necessary to observe one caution, and that is that, when different societies are involved, they should be compared in the same stages of their development.

In a brief conclusion Durkheim summarizes the main points he has made in this little book, a book as important for modern sociology as the *Discourse on Method* of Descartes was to modern philosophy. He wanted first of all to insist that sociology is entirely independent of philosophy and that an independent sociology can in fact contribute more to philosophy than a dependent sociology could. Second, he urged that the method of sociology be an objective method, dominated by the notion that social facts are things and should be treated as things. In the third place, this method is exclusively *sociological* and depends upon no other science. Sociology is an autonomous discipline, accepting when necessary principles discovered in other sciences but never ancillary to them in either method or conclusion. "The feeling of the specificity of social reality is indeed so necessary to the sociologist that only distinctly sociological training can prepare him to grasp social facts intelligently."* The time has come for sociology to proclaim its maturity, to have done with doctrinal disputes, and to take its place—an independent and mature place—among the sciences.

What we have called in the preceding paragraph Durkheim's "little book" can be seen in summary to be a very big book indeed. If many of its conclusions seem no more than common sense today, it has to be remarked that they are common sense precisely because someone made a case for them when they were uncommon sense. The notion that sociology could be a science was not, after all, a widely held notion in Durkheim's day. There was in fact considerable hostility to it. Until Durkheim accepted the chair of social science at Bordeaux in 1887, there was no professorship, no department, and no curriculum of sociology in all of France. Nor, for that matter, did such chairs exist anywhere else. Durkheim was in a very real sense a pioneer in a world movement toward the establishment of a science of sociology, and his book on method was a manifesto that declared to all who could read that a science of sociology was not only possible, it was also necessary.

Sociology is necessary because there is a separate realm of facts—social facts—that are studied by no

Ibid., p. 145.

other science and that are especially different from, and independent of, psychological facts. These social facts are distinguished by two principal criteria, exteriority and constraint. That is, they are exterior to the individual and they constrain him. It may be that Durkheim could have used a different language here, that the words "exteriority" and "constraint" both have negative connotations that he could easily have avoided, and thus ensured a more favorable, or at least a more rapid, reception of his thesis. The same observation applies, as we have suggested, to his use of concepts like the *conscience collective*. We are less afraid of the language now, less suspicious, and less worried about possible metaphysical intrusions into the domain of sociology. But that again is true only because the battles have been won, battles in which Durkheim served as one of the greatest of strategists.

The excerpts that follow, from *The Rules of Sociological Method,* include the whole of Chapter I, "What Is a Social Fact?"; the first two sections of Chapter V, "Rules for the Explanation of Social Facts," in which Durkheim indulges in his most enthusiastic anti-psychological sentiments; and his Conclusion.

What Is a Social Fact? *

Before inquiring into the method suited to the study of social facts, it is important to know which facts are commonly called "social." This information is all the more necessary since the designation "social" is used with little precision. It is currently employed for practically all phenomena generally diffused within society, however small their social interest. But on that basis,

Ibid., pp. 1–13.

there are, as it were, no human events that may not be called social. Each individual drinks, sleeps, eats, reasons; and it is to society's interest that these functions be exercised in an orderly manner. If, then, all these facts are counted as "social" facts, sociology would have no subject matter exclusively its own, and its domain would be confused with that of biology and psychology.

But in reality there is in every society a certain group of phenomena which may be differentiated from those studied by the other natural sciences. When I fulfil my obligations as brother, husband, or citizen, when I execute my contracts, I perform duties which are defined, externally to myself and my acts, in law and in custom. Even if they conform to my own sentiments and I feel their reality subjectively, such reality is still objective, for I did not create them; I merely inherited them through my education. How many times it happens, moreover, that we are ignorant of the details of the obligations incumbent upon us, and that in order to acquaint ourselves with them we must consult the law and its authorized interpreters! Similarly, the church-member finds the beliefs and practices of his religious life ready-made at birth; their existence prior to his own implies their existence outside of himself. The system of signs I use to express my thought, the system of currency I employ to pay my debts, the instruments of credit I utilize in my commercial relations, the practices followed in my profession, etc., function independently of my own use of them. And these statements can be repeated for each member of society. Here, then, are ways of acting, thinking, and feeling that present the noteworthy property of existing outside the individual consciousness.

These types of conduct or thought are not only external to the individual but are, moreover, endowed with coercive power by virtue of which they impose themselves upon him, independent of his individual will. Of course, when I fully consent and conform to them, this constraint is felt only slightly, if at all, and is therefore unnecessary. But it is, nonetheless, an intrinsic characteristic of these facts, the proof thereof being that it asserts itself as soon as I attempt to resist it. If I attempt to violate the law, it reacts against me so as to prevent my act before its accomplishment, or to nullify my violation by restoring the damage, if it is accomplished and reparable, or to make me expiate it if it cannot be compensated for otherwise.

In the case of purely moral maxims, the public conscience exercises a check on every act which offends it by means of the surveillance it exercises over the conduct of citizens, and the appropriate penalties at its disposal. In many cases the constraint is less violent, but nevertheless it always exists. If I do not submit to the conventions of society, if in my dress I do not conform to the customs observed in my country and in my class, the ridicule I provoke, the social isolation in which I am kept, produce, although in an attenuated form, the same effects as a punishment in the strict sense of the word. The constraint is nonetheless efficacious for being indirect. I am not obliged to speak French with my fellow-countrymen nor to use the legal currency, but I cannot possibly do otherwise. If I tried to escape this necessity, my attempt would fail miserably. As an industrialist, I am free to apply the technical methods of former centuries; but by doing so, I should invite certain ruin. Even when I free myself from these rules and violate them successfully, I am always compelled to struggle with them. When finally overcome, they make their constraining power sufficiently felt by the resistance they offer. The enterprises of all innovators, including successful ones, come up against resistance of this kind.

Here, then, is a category of facts with very distinctive characteristics: it consists of ways of acting, thinking, and feeling, external to the individual, and endowed with a power of coercion, by reason of which they control him. These ways of thinking could not be confused with biological phenomena, since they consist of representations and of actions; nor with psychological phenomena, which exist only in the individual consciousness and through it. They constitute, thus, a new variety of phenomena; and it is to them exclusively that the term "social" ought to be applied. And this term fits them quite well, for it is clear that, since their source is not in the individual, their substratum can be no other than society, either the political society as a whole or some one of the partial groups it includes, such as religious denominations, political, literary, and occupational associations, etc. On the other hand, this term "social" applies to them exclusively, for it has a distinct meaning only if it designates exclusively the phenomena which are not included in any of the categories of facts that have already been established and classified. These ways of thinking and acting therefore constitute the proper domain of sociology. It is true that, when we define them with this word "constraint," we risk shocking the zealous partisans of absolute individualism. For those who profess the complete autonomy of the individual, man's dignity is diminished whenever he is made to feel that he is not completely self-determinant. It is generally accepted today, however, that most of our ideas and our tendencies are not developed by ourselves but come to us from without. How can they become a part of us except by imposing themselves upon us? This is the whole meaning of our definition. And it is generally accepted, moreover, that social constraint is not necessarily incompatible with the individual personality.

Since the examples that we have just cited (legal and moral regulations, religious faiths, financial systems, etc.) all consist of established beliefs and practices, one might be led to believe that social facts exist only where there is some social organization. But there are other

facts without such crystallized form which have the
same objectivity and the same ascendency over the individual. These are called "social currents." Thus the
great movements of enthusiasm, indignation, and pity
in a crowd do not originate in any one of the particular
individual consciousnesses. They come to each one of
us from without and can carry us away in spite of ourselves. Of course, it may happen that, in abandoning
myself to them unreservedly, I do not feel the pressure
they exert upon me. But it is revealed as soon as I try to
resist them. Let an individual attempt to oppose one of
these collective manifestations, and the emotions that
he denies will turn against him. Now, if this power of
external coercion asserts itself so clearly in cases of resistance, it must exist also in the first-mentioned cases,
although we are unconscious of it. We are then victims
of the illusion of having ourselves created that which
actually forced itself from without. If the complacency
with which we permit ourselves to be carried along con-
ceals the pressure undergone, nevertheless it does not
abolish it. Thus, air is no less heavy because we do not
detect its weight. So, even if we ourselves have spontaneously contributed to the production of the common
emotion, the impression we have received differs
markedly from that which we would have experienced
if we had been alone. Also, once the crowd has dispersed, that is, once these social influences have ceased
to act upon us and we are alone again, the emotions
which have passed through the mind appear strange to
us, and we no longer recognize them as ours. We realize
that these feelings have been impressed upon us to a
much greater extent that they were created by us. It
may even happen that they horrify us, so much were
they contrary to our nature. Thus, a group of individuals, most of whom are perfectly inoffensive, may,
when gathered in a crowd, be drawn into acts of atroc-
ity. And what we say of these transitory outbursts applies similarly to those more permanent currents of

opinion on religious, political, literary, or artistic matters which are constantly being formed around us, whether in society as a whole or in more limited circles.

To confirm this definition of the social fact by a characteristic illustration from common experience, one need only observe the manner in which children are brought up. Considering the facts as they are and as they have always been, it becomes immediately evident that all education is a continuous effort to impose on the child ways of seeing, feeling, and acting which he could not have arrived at spontaneously. From the very first hours of his life, we compel him to eat, drink, and sleep at regular hours; we constrain him to cleanliness, calmness, and obedience; later we exert pressure upon him in order that he may learn proper consideration for others, respect for customs and conventions, the need for work, etc. If, in time, this constraint ceases to be felt, it is because it gradually gives rise to habits and to internal tendencies that render constraint unnecessary; but nevertheless it is not abolished, for it is still the source from which these habits were derived. It is true that, acccording to Spencer, a rational education ought to reject such methods, allowing the child to act in complete liberty; but as this pedagogic theory has never been applied by any known people, it must be accepted only as an expression of personal opinion, not as a fact which can contradict the aforementioned observations. What makes these facts particularly instructive is that the aim of education is, precisely, the socialization of the human being; the process of education, therefore, gives us in a nutshell the historical fashion in which the social being is constituted. This unremitting pressure to which the child is subjected is the very pressure of the social milieu which tends to fashion him in its own image, and of which parents and teachers are merely the representatives and intermediaries.

It follows that sociological phenomena cannot be

defined by their universality. A thought which we find in every individual consciousness, a movement repeated by all individuals, is not thereby a social fact. If sociologists have been satisfied with defining them by this characteristic, it is because they confused them with what one might call their reincarnation in the individual. It is, however, the collective aspects of the beliefs, tendencies, and practices of a group that characterize truly social phenomena. As for the forms that the collective states assume when refracted in the individual, these are things of another sort. This duality is clearly demonstrated by the fact that these two orders of phenomena are frequently found dissociated from one another. Indeed, certain of these social manners of acting and thinking acquire, by reason of their repetition, a certain rigidity which on its own account crystallizes them, so to speak, and isolates them from the particular events which reflect them. They thus acquire a body, a tangible form, and constitute a reality in their own right, quite distinct from the individual facts which produce it. Collective habits are inherent not only in the successive acts which they determine but, by a privilege of which we find no example in the biological realm, they are given permanent expression in a formula which is repeated from mouth to mouth, transmitted by education, and fixed even in writing. Such is the origin and nature of legal and moral rules, popular aphorisms and proverbs, articles of faith wherein religious or political groups condense their beliefs, standards of taste established by literary schools, etc. None of these can be found entirely reproduced in the applications made of them by individuals since they can exist even without being actually applied.

No doubt, this dissociation does not always manifest itself with equal distinctness, but its obvious existence in the important and numerous cases just cited is sufficient to prove that the social fact is a thing distinct from its individual manifestations. Moreover, even when this dissociation is not immediately apparent, it may often be disclosed by certain devices of method. Such dissociation is indispensable if one wishes to separate social facts from their alloys in order to observe them in a state of purity. Currents of opinion, with an intensity varying according to the time and place, impel certain groups either to more marriages, for example, or to more suicides, or to a higher or lower birthrate, etc. These currents are plainly social facts. At first sight they seem inseparable from the forms they take in individual cases. But statistics furnish us with the means of isolating them. They are, in fact, represented with considerable exactness by the rates of births, marriages, and suicides, that is, by the number obtained by dividing the average annual total of marriages, births, suicides, by the number of persons whose ages lie within the range in which marriages, births, and suicides occur. Since each of these figures contains all the individual cases indiscriminately, the individual circumstances which may have had a share in the production of the phenomenon are neutralized and, consequently, do not contribute to its determination. The average, then, expresses a certain state of the group mind [*l'âme collective*].

Such are social phenomena, when disentangled from all foreign matter. As for their individual manifestations, these are indeed, to a certain extent, social, since they partly reproduce a social model. Each of them also depends, and to a large extent, on the organopsychological constitution of the individual and on the particular circumstances in which he is placed. Thus they are not sociological phenomena in the strict sense of the word. They belong to two realms at once; one could call them sociopsychological. They interest the sociologist without constituting the immediate subject matter of sociology. There exist in the interior of organisms similar phenomena, compound in their nature, which form in their turn the subject matter of the "hybrid sciences," such as physiological chemistry, for example.

The objection may be raised that a phenomenon is collective only if it is common to all members of society, or at least to most of them—in other words, if it is truly general. This may be true; but it is general because it is collective (that is, more or less obligatory), and certainly not collective because general. It is a group condition repeated in the individual because imposed on him. It is to be found in each part because it exists in the whole, rather than in the whole because it exists in the parts. This becomes conspicuously evident in those beliefs and practices which are transmitted to us ready-made by previous generations; we receive and adopt them because, being both collective and ancient, they are invested with a particular authority that education has taught us to recognize and respect. It is, of course, true that a vast portion of our social culture is transmitted to us in this way; but even when the social fact is due in part to our direct collaboration, its nature is not different. A collective emotion which bursts forth suddenly and violently in a crowd does not express merely what all the individual sentiments had in common; it is something entirely different, as we have shown. It results from their being together, a product of the actions and reactions which take place between individual consciousnesses; and if each individual consciousness echoes the collective sentiment, it is by virtue of the special energy resident in its collective origin. If all hearts beat in unison, this is not the result of a spontaneous and pre-established harmony but rather because an identical force propels them in the same direction. Each is carried along by all.

We thus arrive at the point where we can formulate and delimit in a precise way the domain of sociology. It comprises only a limited group of phenomena. A social fact is to be recognized by the power of external coercion which it exercises or is capable of exercising over individuals, and the presence of this power may be recognized in its turn either by the existence of some specific sanction or by the resistance offered against every individual effort that tends to violate it. One can, however, define it also by its diffusion. This last criterion is perhaps, in certain cases, easier to apply than the preceding one. In fact, the constraint is easy to ascertain when it expresses itself externally by some direct reaction of society, as is the case in law, morals, beliefs, customs, and even fashions. But when it is only indirect, like the constraint which an economic organization exercises, it cannot always be so easily detected. Generality combined with externality may, then, be easier to establish. Moreover, this second definition is but another form of the first; for if a mode of behavior whose existence is external to individual consciousnesses becomes general, this can only be brought about by its being imposed upon them.

But these several phenomena present the same characteristic by which we defined the others. These "ways of existing" are imposed on the individual precisely in the same fashion as the "ways of acting" of which we have spoken. Indeed, when we wish to know how a society is divided politically, of what these divisions themselves are composed, and how complete is the fusion existing between them, we shall not achieve our purpose by physical inspection and by geographical observations; for these phenomena are social, even when they have some basis in physical nature. It is only by a study of public law that a comprehension of this organization is possible, for it is this law that determines the organization, as it equally determines our domestic and civil relations. This political organization is, then, no less obligatory than the social facts mentioned above. If the population crowds into our cities instead of scattering into the country, this is due to a trend of public opinion, a collective drive that imposes this concentration upon the individuals. We can no more choose the style of our houses than of our clothing—at least, both are equally obligatory. The channels of communication prescribe the direction of internal migrations and commerce, etc., and even their extent. Consequently, at the very most, it should be necessary to add to the list of phenomena which we have enumerated as presenting the distinctive criterion of a social fact only one additional category, "ways of existing"; and, as this enumeration was not meant to be rigorously exhaustive, the addition would not be absolutely necessary.

Such an addition is perhaps not necessary, for these "ways of existing" are only crystallized "ways of acting." The political structure of a society is merely the way in which its component segments have become accustomed to live with one another. If their relations are traditionally intimate, the segments tend to fuse with one another, or, in the contrary case, to retain their identity. The type of habitation imposed upon us is merely the way in which our contemporaries and our ancestors have been accustomed to construct their houses. The methods of communication are merely the channels which the regular currents of commerce and migrations have dug, by flowing in the same direction. To be sure, if the phenomena of a structural character alone presented this permanence, one might believe that they constituted a distinct species. A legal regulation is an arrangement no less permanent than a type of architecture, and yet the regulation is a "physiological" fact. A simple moral maxim is assuredly somewhat more malleable, but it is much more rigid than a simple professional custom or a fashion. There is thus a whole series of degrees without a break in continuity between the facts of the most articulated structure and those free currents of social life which are not yet definitely molded. The differences between them are, therefore, only differences in the degree of consolidation they present. Both are simply life, more or less crystallized. No doubt, it may be of some advantage to serve the term "morphological" for those social facts which concern the social substratum, but only on condition of not overlooking the fact that they are of the same nature as the others. Our definition will then include the whole relevant range of facts if we say: A social fact is every way of acting, fixed or not, capable of exercising on the individual an external constraint; or again, every way of acting which is general throughout a given society, while at the same time existing in its own right independent of its individual manifestations.

Rules for the Explanation of Social Facts*

The establishment of species is, above all, a means of grouping facts in order to facilitate their interpretation. But social morphology is only an introduction to the truly explanatory part of the science. What is the proper method of this part?

I Most sociologists think they have accounted for phenomena once they have shown how they are useful, what role they play, reasoning as if facts existed only from the point of view of this role and with no other determining cause than the sentiment, clear or confused, of the services they are called to render. That is why they think they have said all that is necessary, to render them intelligible, when they have established the reality of these services and have shown what social needs they satisfy.

Thus Comte traces the entire progressive force of the human species to his fundamental tendency "which directly impels man constantly to ameliorate his condi-

*Ibid., pp. 89–112.

tion, whatever it may be, under all circumstances," and Spencer relates this force to the need for greater happiness. It is in accordance with this principle that Spencer explains the formation of society by the alleged advantages which result from cooperation; the institution of government, by the utility of the regularization of military cooperation; the transformations through which the family has passed, by the need for reconciling more and more perfectly the interests of parents, children, and society.

But this method confuses two very different questions. To show how a fact is useful is not to explain how it originated or why it is what it is. The uses which it serves presuppose the specific properties characterizing it but do not create them. The need we have of things cannot give them existence, nor can it confer their specific nature upon them. It is to causes of another sort that they owe their existence. The idea we have of their utility may indeed motivate us to put these forces to work and to elicit from them their characteristic effects, but it will not enable us to produce these effects out of nothing. This proposition is evident so long as it is a question only of material, or even psychological, phenomena. It would be equally evident in sociology if social facts, because of their extreme intangibility, did not wrongly appear to us as without all intrinsic reality. Since we usually see them as a product purely of mental effort, it seems to us that they may be produced at will whenever we find it necessary. But since each one of them is a force, superior to that of the individual, and since it has a separate existence, it is not true that merely by willing to do so may one call them into being. No force can be engendered except by an antecedent force. To revive the spirit of the family, where it has become weakened, it is not enough that everyone understand its advantages; the causes which alone can engender it must be made to act directly. To give a government the authority necessary for it, it is not enough to feel the need for this authority; we must have recourse to the only sources from which all authority is derived. We must, namely, establish traditions, a common spirit, etc.; and for this it is necessary again to go back along the chain of causes and effects until we find a point where the action of man may be effectively brought to bear.

What shows plainly the dualism of these two orders of research is that a fact can exist without being at all useful, either because it has never been adjusted to any vital end or because, after having been useful, it has lost all utility while continuing to exist by the inertia of habit alone. There are, indeed, more survivals in society than in biological organisms. There are even cases where a practice or a social institution changes its function without thereby changing its nature. The rule, *Is pater quem justae nuptiae declarant,* has remained in our code essentially the same as it was in the old Roman law. While its purpose then was to safeguard the property rights of a father over children born to the legitimate wife, it is rather the rights of children that it protects today. The custom of taking an oath began by being a sort of judiciary test and has become today simply a solemn and imposing formality. The religious dogmas of Christianity have not changed for centuries, but the role which they play is not the same in our modern societies as in the Middle Ages. Thus, the same words may serve to express new ideas. It is, moreover, a proposition true in sociology, as in biology, that the organ is independent of the function—in other words, while remaining the same, it can serve different ends. The causes of its existence are, then, independent of the ends it serves.

Nevertheless, we do not mean to say that the impulses, needs, and desires of men never intervene actively in social evolution. On the contrary, it is certain that they can hasten or retard its development, according to the circumstances which determine the social phenomena. Apart from the fact that they cannot, in any case, make something out of nothing, their actual intervention, whatever may be its effects, can take place only by means of efficient causes. A deliberate intention can contribute, even in this limited way, to the production of a new phenomenon only if it has itself been newly formed or if it is itself a result of some transformation of a previous intention. For, unless we postulate a truly providential and pre-established harmony, we cannot admit that man has carried with him from the beginning —potentially ready to be awakened at the call of circumstances—all the intentions which conditions were destined to demand in the course of human evolution. It must further be recognized that a deliberate intention is itself something objectively real; it can, then, neither be created nor modified by the mere fact that we judge it useful. It is a force having a nature of its own; for that nature to be given existence or altered, it is not enough that we should find this advantageous. In order to bring about such changes, there must be a sufficient cause.

For example, we have explained the constant development of the division of labor by showing that it is necessary in order that man may maintain himself in the new conditions of existence as he advances in history. We have attributed to this tendency, which is rather improperly named the "instinct of self-preservation," an important role in our explanations. But, in the first place, this instinct alone could not account for even the most rudimentary specialization. It can do nothing if the conditions on which the division of labor depends do not already exist, i.e., if individual differences have not increased sufficiently as a consequence of the progressive disintegration of the common consciousness and of hereditary influences. It was even necessary that division of labor should have already begun to exist for its usefulness to be seen and for the need of it to make itself felt. The very development of individual differences, necessarily accompanied by a greater diversity of tastes and aptitudes, produced this first result. Further, the instinct of self-preservation did not, of itself and without cause, come to fertilize this first germ of specialization. We were started in this new direction, first, because the course we previously followed was now barred and because the greater intensity of the struggle, owing to the more extensive consolidation of societies, made more and more difficult the survival of individuals who continued to devote themselves to unspecialized tasks. For such reasons it became necessary for us to change our mode of living. Moreover, if our activity has been turned toward a constantly more developed division of labor, it is because this was also the direction of least resistance. The other possible solutions were emigration, suicide, and crime. Now, in the average case, the ties attaching us to life and country and the sympathy we have for our fellows are sentiments stronger and more resistant than the habits which could deflect us from narrower specialization. These habits, then, had inevitably to yield to each impulse that arose. Thus the fact that we allow a place for human needs in sociological explanations does not mean that we even partially revert to teleology. These needs can influence social evolution only on condition that they themselves, and the changes they undergo, can be explained solely by causes that are deterministic and not at all purposive.

But what is even more convincing than the preceding considerations is a study of actual social behavior. Where purpose reigns, there reigns also a more or less wide contingency; for there are no ends, and even fewer means, which necessarily control all men, even when it is assumed that they are placed in the same circumstances. Given the same environment, each individual adapts himself to it according to his own disposition and in his own way, which he prefers to all other ways. One person will seek to change it and make it conform to his needs; another will prefer to change himself and moderate his desires. To arrive at the same goal many different ways can be and actually are followed. If, then, it were true that historic development took place in terms of ends clearly or obscurely felt, social facts should present the most infinite diversity; and all comparison should be almost impossible.

To be sure, the external events which constitute the superficial part of social life vary from one people to another just as each individual has his own history, although the bases of physical and moral organization are the same for all. But when one comes in contact with social phenomena, one is, on the contrary, surprised by the astonishing regularity with which they occur under the same circumstances. Even the most minute and the most trivial practices recur with the most astonishing uniformity. A certain nuptial ceremony, purely symbolical in appearance, such as the carrying-off of the betrothed, is found to be exactly the same wherever a certain family type exists; and again this family type itself is linked to a whole social organization. The most bizarre customs, such as the couvade, the levirate, exogamy, etc., are observed among the most diverse peoples and are symptomatic of a certain social state. The right to make one's will appears at a certain phase of history, and the more or less important restrictions limiting it offer a fairly exact clue to the particular stage of social evolution. It would be easy to multiply examples. This wide diffusion of collective forms would be inexplicable if purpose or final causes had the predominant place in sociology that is attributed to them.

When, then, the explanation of a social phenomenon is undertaken, we must seek separately the efficient cause which produces it and the function it fulfils. We use the word "function," in preference to "end" or "purpose," precisely because social phenomena do not generally exist for the useful results they produce. We must determine whether there is a correspondence between the fact under consideration and the general needs of the social organism, and in what this correspondence consists, without occupying ourselves with whether it has been intentional or not. All these questions of intention are too subjective to allow of scientific treatment.

Not only must these two types of problems be separated, but it is proper, in general, to treat the former before the latter. This sequence, indeed, corresponds to that of experience. It is natural to seek the causes of a phenomenon before trying to determine its effects. This method is all the more logical since the first question, once answered, will often help to answer the second. Indeed, the bond which unites the cause to the effect is reciprocal to an extent which has not been sufficiently recognized. The effect can doubtless not exist without its cause; but the latter, in turn, needs its effect. It is from the cause that the effect draws its energy; but it also restores it to the cause on occasion, and consequently it cannot disappear without the cause showing the effects of its disappearance.

For example, the social reaction that we call "punishment" is due to the intensity of the collective sentiments which the crime offends; but, from another angle, it has the useful function of maintaining these sentiments at the same degree of intensity, for they would soon diminish if offenses against them were not punished. Similarly, in proportion as the social milieu becomes more complex and more unstable, traditions and conventional beliefs are shaken, become more indeterminate and more unsteady, and reflective powers are developed. Such rationality is indispensable to societies and individuals in adapting themselves to a more mobile and more complex environment. And again, in proportion as men are obliged to furnish more highly specialized work, the products of this work are multiplied and are of better quality; but this increase in products and improvement in quality are necessary to compensate for the expense which this more considerable work entails. Thus, instead of the cause of social phenomena consisting of a mental anticipation of the function they are called to fill, this function, on the contrary, at least in a number of cases, serves to maintain the pre-existent cause from which they are derived. We shall, then, find the function more easily if the cause is already known.

If the determination of function is thus to be delayed, it is still no less necessary for the complete explanation of the phenomena. Indeed, if the usefulness of a fact is not because of its existence, it is generally necessary that it be useful in order that it may maintain itself. For the fact that it is not useful suffices to make it harmful, since in that case it costs effort without bringing in any returns. If, then, the majority of social phenomena had this parasitic character, the budget of the organism would have a deficit and social life would be impossible. Consequently, to have a satisfactory understanding of the latter, it is necessary to show how the phenomena comprising it combine in such a way as to put society in harmony with itself and with the environment external to it. No doubt, the current formula, which defines social life as a correspondence between the internal and the external milieu, is only an approximation; however, it is in general true. Consequently, to explain a social fact it is not enough to show the cause on which it depends; we must also, at least in most cases, show its function in the establishment of social order.

II Having distinguished between these two approaches, we must determine the method by which they may be developed. At the same time that it is teleological, the method of explanation generally followed by sociologists is essentially psychological. These two tendencies are interconnected with one another. In fact, if society is only a system of means instituted by men to attain certain ends, these ends can only be individual, for only individuals could have existed before society. From the individual, then, have emanated the needs and desires determining the formation of societies; and, if it is from him that all comes, it is necessarily by him that all must be explained. Moreover, there are in societies only individual consciousnesses; in these, then, is found the source of all social evolution.

Hence, sociological laws can be only a corollary of the more general laws of psychology; the ultimate explanation of collective life will consist in showing how it emanates from human nature in general, whether the collective life be deduced from human nature directly and without previous observation or whether it must be related to human nature after the latter has been analyzed.

These terms are almost literally those used by Auguste Comte to characterize his method. "Since," says he, "the social phenomenon, conceived in its totality, is fundamentally only a simple development of humanity, without the creation of any special faculties whatsoever, as I have established above, all the effective dispositions that sociological investigation will successively discover will therefore be found at least in the germ in this primordial type which biology has constructed in advance for sociology." According to him, the predominant fact in social life is progress; and moreover, progress depends o an exclusively psychological factor, namely, the tendency which impels man to perfect his nature more and more. Social facts would then be derived so directly from human nature that during the first phases of history they might be directly deduced from it without the necessity of having recourse to the observation of society. It is true that, as Comte confesses, it is impossible to apply this deductive method to the more advanced periods of evolution. But this impossibility is purely a practical one. It is due to the fact that the distance between the point of departure and the point of arrival becomes so considerable that the human mind risks going astray, if it undertakes to traverse it without a guide. But the relation between the fundamental laws of human nature and the ultimate products of social progress does not cease to be intimate. The most complex forms of civilization are only a development of the psychological life of the individual. Thus, while the theories of psychology are insufficient as premises for sociological reasoning, they are the touchstone which alone can test the validity of propositions inductively established. "A law of social succession," says Comte, "even when indicated with all possible authority by the historical method, ought to be finally admitted only after having been rationally related to the positive theory of human nature, either in a direct or indirect way." Psychology, then, will always have the last word.

Such is likewise the method followed by Spencer. Indeed, according to him, the two primary factors of social phenomena are the external environment and the physical and social constitution of the individual. Now, the former can influence society only through the latter, which thus becomes the essential force of social evolution. If society is formed, it is in order to permit the individual to express his nature; and all the transformations through which this nature has passed have no other object than to make this expression easier and more complete. It is by reason of this principle that, before proceeding to his research in social organization, Spencer thought it necessary to devote almost the entire first volume of his *Principles of Sociology* to the study of the physical, emotional, and intellectual aspects of primitive man. "The science of sociology," he says, "sets out with social units, conditioned as we have seen, constituted physically, emotionally, and intellectually, and possessed of certain early acquired notions and correlative feelings." And it is in two of these feelings—fear of the living and fear of the dead—that he finds the origin of political and religious government. He admits, it is true, that once it is formed society reacts on individuals. But it does not follow that society itself has the power of directly engendering the smallest social fact; from this point of view it exerts an effect only by the intermediation of the changes it effects in the individual. It is, then, always in human nature, whether original or acquired, that everything is based. Moreover, this action that the social body exercises on its members cannot be at all specific, since political ends have no separate existence but are simply a summary statement of human needs. It can then be only a duplication of private activity. In industrial societies, particularly, we are unable to see where social influence has a place, since the object of these societies is, precisely, to liberate the individual and his natural impulses by ridding him of all social constraint.

This principle is not only at the basis of these great doctrines of general sociology, but it likewise fathers an equally large number of specific theories. Thus, domestic organization is commonly explained by the sentiment parents have for their children, and children for their parents; the institution of marriage, by the advantages it presents for the married pair and their progeny; punishment, by the anger which every grave attack upon his interests causes in the individual. All economic life, as economists of the orthodox school especially conceive and explain it, is definitely dependent upon a purely individual factor, the desire for wealth. In morality, the duty of the individual toward himself is made the basis of all ethics. As for religion, it becomes a product of the impressions which the great forces of nature or of certain eminent personalities awaken in man, etc.

But, if such a method is applied to social phenomena, it changes fundamentally their nature. To prove this, let us recall the definition we have given. Since their essential characteristic is their power of exerting pressure on individual consciousnesses, it follows that they are not derived from the latter and, consequently, that sociology is not a corollary of individual psychology. For this power of constraint is evidence of the fact that social phenomena possess a different nature from ours, since they control us only by force or, at the very least, by weighing upon us more or less heavily. If social life were merely an extension of the individual being, it would not thus ascend toward its source, namely, the individual, and impetuously invade it. If the authority before which the individual bows when he acts, feels, or thinks socially governs him to this extent, it does so because it is a product of social forces which transcend him and for which he, consequently, cannot account. The external impulse to which he submits cannot come from him, nor can it be explained by what happens within him. It is true that we are not incapable of self-control; we can restrain our impulses, habits, and even instincts, and can arrest their development by an act of inhibition. But these inhibitory movements should not be confused with those constituting social constraint. The process of the former is centrifugal; of the latter, centripetal. The former are elaborated in the individual consciousness and then tend to externalize themselves; the latter are at first external to the individual, whom they tend to fashion in their image from without. Inhibition is, if you like, the means by which social constraint produces its pychological effects; it is not identical with this constraint.

When the individual has been eliminated, society alone remains. We must, then, seek the explanation of social life in the nature of society itself. It is quite evident that, since it infinitely surpasses the individual in time as well as in space, it is in a position to impose upon him ways of acting and thinking which it has consecrated with its prestige. This pressure, which is the distinctive property of social facts, is the pressure which the totality exerts on the individual.

But, it will be said that, since the only elements making up society are individuals, the first origins of sociological phenomena cannot but be psychological. In reasoning thus, it can be established just as easily that organic phenomena may be explained by inorganic phenomena. It is very certain that there are in the living cell only molecules of crude matter. But these molecules are in contact with one another, and this association is the cause of the new phenomena which characterize life, the very germ of which cannot possibly be found in any of the separate elements. A whole is not identical with the sum of its parts. It is something different, and its properties differ from those of its component parts. Association is not, as has sometimes been believed, merely an infertile phenomenon; it is not simply the putting of facts and constituent properties into juxtaposition. On the contrary, it is the source of all the innovations which have been produced successively in the course of the general evolution of things. What differences are there between the lower and higher organisms, between highly organized living things and protoplasm, between the latter and the inorganic molecules of which it is composed, if not differences in types of association? All these beings, in the last analysis, resolve themselves into the same elements, but these elements are here in mere juxtaposition, there in combination, here associated in one way, there in another. One may even inquire whether this law does not apply in the mineral world and whether the differences separating inorganic bodies are not traceable to this same origin.

By reason of this principle, society is not a mere sum of individuals. Rather, the system formed by their association represents a specific reality which has its own characteristics. Of course, nothing collective can be produced if individual consciousnesses are not assumed; but this necessary condition is by itself insufficient. These consciousnesses must be combined in a certain way; social life results from this combination and is, consequently, explained by it. Individual minds, forming groups by mingling and fusing, give birth to a being, psychological if you will, but constituting a psychic individuality of a new sort. It is, then, in the nature of this collective individuality, not in that of the associated units, that we must seek the immediate and determining causes of the facts appearing therein. The group thinks, feels, and acts quite differently from the way in which its members would were they isolated. If, then, we begin with the individual, we shall be able to understand nothing of what takes place in the group. In a word, there is between psychology and sociology the same break in continuity as between biology and the physicochemical sciences. Consequently, every time that a social phenomenon is directly explained by a psychological phenomenon, we may be sure that the explanation is false.

Our critics will perhaps maintain that although society, once formed, is the proximate cause of social phenomena, the causes determining its formation may still be psychological in nature. They grant that, when individuals are associated, their association can give rise to a new form of life; but they claim that the new form can take place only for reasons inherent in individuals. But, in reality, as far back as one goes in history, the principle of association is the most imperative of all, for it is the source of all other compulsions. As a consequence of my birth, I am obliged to associate with a given group. It may be said that later, as an adult, I acquiesce in this obligation by the very fact that I continue to live in my country. But what difference does that make? This "acquiescence" is still imperative. Pressure accepted and submitted to with good grace is still pressure. Moreover, let us look more closely at the nature of my acquiescence. For the present, it is most certainly imposed upon me, for in the vast majority of cases it is materially and morally impossible for us to strip off our nationality; such a change is generally considered apostasy. Likewise in the past, which determines the present, I could not have given my free consent. I did not desire the education I received, which, more than any other thing, fixes me to my native soil. Finally, for the future, I cannot give my acquiescence, for I cannot know what the future is to be. I do not know all the duties which may be incumbent upon me at some future time in my capacity as a citizen. How could I acquiesce in them in advance?

We have shown, then, that the source of all that is obligatory is outside the individual. So long, then, as we do not desert the facts, the principle of association presents the same character as the others and, consequently, is explained in the same manner.

Moreover, as all societies are born of other societies without a break in continuity, we can be certain that in the entire course of social evolution there has not been a single time when individuals determined by careful deliberation whether or not they would enter into the collective life or into one collective life rather than another. In order for that question to arise, it would be necessary to go back to the first origins of all societies. But the questionable solutions which can be brought to such problems could not, in any case, affect the method by which we must treat the facts given in history. Therefore, we do not need to discuss them.

But one would be strangely mistaken about our thought if, from the foregoing, he drew the conclusion that sociology, according to us, must, or even can, make an abstraction of man and his faculties. It is clear, on the contrary, that the general characteristics of human nature participate in the work of elaboration from which social life results. But they are not the cause of it, nor do they give it its special form; they only make it possible. Collective representations, emotions, and tendencies are caused not by certain states of the consciousnesses of individuals but by the conditions in which the social group in its totality is placed. Such actions can, of course, materialize only if the individual natures are not resistant to them; but these individual natures are merely the indeterminate material that the social factor molds and transforms. Their contribution consists exclusively in very general attitudes, in vague and consequently plastic predispositions which, by themselves, if other agents did not intervene, could not take on the definite and complex forms which characterize social phenomena.

What an abyss, for example, between the sentiments man experiences in the face of forces superior to his own and the present religious institution with its beliefs, its numerous and complicated practices, its material and moral organization! What a contrast between the psychic states of sympathy which two beings of the same blood experience for one another, and the detailed collection of legal and moral regulations that determine the structure of the family, the relations of persons among themselves, of things with persons, etc.! We have seen that, even where society is reduced to an unorganized crowd, the collective sentiments which are formed in it may not only not resemble, but even be opposed to, the sentiments of the average individual. How much greater must be the difference between them when the pressure exerted on the individual is that of a well-organized society, in which the action of the traditions of former generations is added to that of contemporaries! A purely psychological explanation of social facts cannot fail, therefore, to allow all that is characteristic (i.e., social) in them to escape.

What has blinded most sociologists to the inadequacy of this method is that, taking effect for cause, they have very often designated as determining the conditions of social phenomena certain psychological states that are relatively definite and distinctive but which are, after all, only the consequence of these social phenomena. Thus a certain religious sentiment has been considered innate in man, a certain minimum of sexual jealousy, filial piety, paternal love, etc. And it is by these that religion, marriage, and the family have been explained.

History, however, shows that these inclinations, far from being inherent in human nature, are often totally lacking. Or they may present such variations in different societies that the residue obtained after eliminating all these differences—which alone can be considered of psychological origin—is reduced to something vague and rudimentary and far removed from the facts that need explanation. These sentiments, then, result from the collective organization and are not its basis. It has not been proved at all that the tendency to gregariousness has been an inherited instinct of the human species from its beginnings. It is much more natural to consider it a product of social life, which was slowly developed within us; for it is a fact of observation that animals are or are not gregarious according to whether their habits oblige them to live a common life or to avoid it. We must add that the difference between even the more definite tendencies and social reality remains considerable.

There is, moreover, a way to isolate the psychological factor almost completely in such a manner as to determine precisely the extent of its action, viz., to see how race affects social evolution. Indeed, ethnic characteristics are organicopsychological in type. Social life must, therefore, vary when they vary, if psychological phenomena have on society the effects attributed to them. But no social phenomenon is known which can be placed in indisputable dependence on race. No doubt, we cannot attribute to this proposition the value of a principle; we can merely affirm it as invariably true in practical experience.

The most diverse forms of organization are found in societies of the same race, while striking similarities are observed between societies of different races. The city-state existed among the Phoenicians, as among the Romans and the Greeks; we find it in the process of formation among the Kabyles. The patriarchal family was almost as highly developed among the Jews as among the Hindus; but it is not found among the Slavs, who are, however, of the Aryan race. On the other hand, the family type met among Slavs also exists among the Arabs. The maternal family and the clan are observed everywhere. The detail of legal procedure and of nuptial ceremonies is the same among peoples most dissimilar from the ethnic point of view.

If all these things are true, it is because the psychological factor is too general to predetermine the course of social phenomena. Since it does not call for one social form rather than another, it cannot explain any of them. There are, it is true, a certain number of facts which are customarily attributed to the influence of race. In this manner is explained, notably, the rapid and intensive development of arts and letters in Athens, so slow and mediocre in Rome. But this interpretation of the facts, although classical, has never been scientifically demonstrated; it seems, indeed, to derive all its authority solely from tradition. The possibility of a sociological explanation of the same phenomena has not been explored, but we are convinced that it could be attempted with success. In short, when the artistic character of Athenian civilization is related with such facility to inherited aesthetic faculties, we show as little insight as did scholars in the Middle Ages when they explained fire by phlogiston and the effects of opium by its dormitive property.

Finally, if social evolution really had its origin in the psychological constitution of man, its origin seems to be completely obscure. For we would then have to admit that its motivating force is some inner spring of human nature. But what could this be? Is it the sort of instinct Comte speaks of, which impels man more and more to express his nature? But that is begging the question and explaining progress by an innate "tendency toward progress"—a metaphysical entity of the very existence of which there is no demonstration. Even the highest animal species are not at all activated by the need to progress, and among human societies there are many which are content to remain indefinitely stationary.

Or is this motivating force, as Spencer seems to believe, the urge for greater happiness which the increasingly complex forms of civilization are designed to satisfy more and more completely? We would then have to establish the fact that happiness increases with civilization, and we have elsewhere described all the difficulties to which this hypothesis gives rise. But further, even if one or the other of these two postulates were admissible, historical development would not thereby be rendered intelligible, for the explanation which would result from it would be purely teleological. We have shown above that social facts, like all natural phenomena, are not explained by the simple consideration that they serve some end. When it has been proved satisfactorily that the progressively more intelligent social organizations which have succeeded one another in the course of history have had the effect of satisfying more and more certain of our fundamental desires, we have not shown at all how these social organizations have been produced. The fact that they were useful does not tell us how they originated. Even if we were to explain how we came to imagine them and how we planned them in advance so as to picture to ourselves their services to us—a somewhat difficult problem in itself—the desires which called forth their existence do not have the power of drawing them out of nothing. In a word, admitting that social organizations are the necessary means to attain a desired goal, the whole question remains: From what source and by what means have these been created?

We arrive, therefore, at the following principle: *The determining cause of a social fact should be sought among the social facts preceding it and not among the states of the individual consciousness.* Moreover, we see quite readily that all the foregoing applies to the determination of the function as well as the cause of social phenomena. The function of a social fact cannot but be social, i.e., it consists of the production of socially useful effects. To be sure, it may and does happen that it also serves the individual. But this happy result is not its immediate cause. We can then complete the preceding proposition by saying: *The function of a social fact ought always to be sought in its relation to some social end*.

Since sociologists have often misinterpreted this rule and have considered social phenomena from a too psychological point of view, to many their theories seem too vague and shifting and too far removed from the distinctive nature of the things they are intended to explain. Historians who treat social reality directly and in detail have not failed to remark how powerless these too general interpretations are to show the relation between the facts; and their mistrust of sociology has been, no doubt, partly produced by this circumstance. We do not mean to say, of course, that the study of psychological facts is not indispensable to the sociologist. If collective life is not derived from individual life, the two are nevertheless closely related; if the latter cannot explain the former, it can at least facilitate its explanation. First, as we have shown, it is indisputable that social facts are produced by action on psychological factors. In addition, this very action is similar to that which takes place in each individual consciousness and by which are transformed the primary elements (sensations, reflexes, instincts) of which it is originally constituted. Not without reason has it been said that the self is itself a society, by the same right as the organism, although in another way; and long ago psychologists showed the great importance of the factor of association in the explanation of mental activity.

Psychological training, more than biological training, constitutes, then, a valuable lesson for the sociologist; but it will not be useful to him except on condition that he emancipates himself from it after having received profit from its lessons, and then goes beyond it by special sociological training. He must abandon psychology as the center of his operations, as the point of departure for his excursions into the sociological world to which they must always return. He must establish himself in the very heart of social facts, in order to observe them directly, while asking the science of the individual mind for a general preparation only and, when needed, for useful suggestions.

Conclusion*

To sum up, the distinctive characteristics of our method are as follows: First, it is entirely independent of philosophy. Because sociology had its birth in the great philosophical system and thus has been continuously overburdened with it, it has been successively positivistic, evolutionary, idealistic, when it should have been content to be simply sociology. We should even hesitate to describe it as naturalistic, unless the term indicates merely that the sociologist considers social facts as capable of being explained naturally, or that he is a scientist and not a mystic. We reject the term if it is given a doctrinal meaning concerning the essence of social objects—if, e.g., by it is meant that social objects are reducible to the other cosmic forces.

Sociology does not need to choose between the great hypotheses which divide metaphysicians. It needs to embrace free will no more than determinism. All that it asks is that the principle of causality be applied to social phenomena. Again, this principle is enunciated for sociology not as a rational necessity but only as an empirical postulate, produced by legitimate induction.

Ibid., pp. 141–46.

Since the law of causality has been verified in the other realms of nature, and since it has progressively extended its authority from the physicochemical world to the biological, and from the latter to the psychological, we are justified in claiming that it is possible to add today that the researches undertaken on the basis of this postulate tend to confirm it. However, the question as to whether the nature of the causal bond excludes all chance is not thereby settled.

This emancipation of sociology is decidedly to the advantage of philosophy. For, in so far as the sociologist has not sufficiently eliminated philosophy from social science, he considers social facts only from their most general aspect, the aspect from which they most resemble the other things in the universe. Now, if sociology, thus conceived, serves to illustrate philosophy with curious facts, it does not enrich it with new views, since it points out nothing new in the objects which it studies. But, if the fundamental facts of the other fields of knowledge actually recur in the social field, they do so under special forms, which clarify the nature of these facts since they are their highest expression. However, in order to treat them from this aspect, we must leave generalities behind and enter into the detail of facts. Thus, as sociology becomes specialized, it will furnish more original materials for philosophical reflection.

All this has already given us an idea of how the essential concepts, such as those of species, organ, function, health and morbidity, cause and effect, appear in sociology under entirely new aspects. Moreover, may not sociology feature an idea which might well be the basis not only of a psychology but of a whole philosophy—the idea of association?

With reference to practical social doctrines, our method permits and commands the same independence. Sociology thus understood will be neither individualistic, communistic, nor socialistic in the sense commonly given these words. On principle, it will ignore these theories, in which it could not recognize any scientific value, since they tend not to describe or interpret, but to reform, social organization. At least, if it takes an interest in them, it is in proportion as it sees in them social facts which can aid it both in understanding the social reality and in disclosing the needs that are the motivating power in society. We do not mean, however, that it ought to take no interest in practical questions. It has been evident, on the contrary, that our constant preoccupation has been to orient it so that it might have practical results. It necessarily meets these problems at the end of its researches. But, by the very fact that they present themselves to sociology only at this moment, and that, consequently, they are derived from facts and not from emotions, one can foresee that they must be formulated for the sociologist in quite other terms than for the masses, and that the tentative solutions it can give them could not coincide exactly with any of those which now satisfy various interest groups. But the role of sociology from this point of view must properly consist in emancipating us from all parties, not to the extent of negating all doctrine, but by persuading us to assume toward these questions a special attitude that science alone can give in its direct contact with things. Science alone can teach us to treat historic institutions, whatever they may be, with respect but without mystic awe, by making us appreciate both their permanent and their ephemeral aspects, their stability and their infinite variability.

In the second place, our method is objective. It is dominated entirely by the idea that social facts are things and must be treated as such. No doubt, this principle is found again, under a slightly different form, at the basis of the doctrines of Comte and Spencer. But these great thinkers gave it theoretic formulation without putting it into practice. In order that it might not remain a dead letter, it is not sufficient to promulgate it; it is necessary to make it the basis of an entire discipline which will take hold of the student at the very moment he approaches the subject of his researches, and which will accompany him, step by step, in all his proceedings. We have devoted ourselves to instituting this discipline.

We have shown how the sociologist has to disregard the preconceptions which he had of facts, in order to face the facts themselves; how he has to discriminate among them according to their most objective characteristics; how he must seek in the facts themselves the means of classifying them as normal and pathological; how, finally, he must be inspired by the same principle in the explanations he attempts as in the way in which he tests these explanations. For, as soon as he has the feeling that he is in the presence of things, he will no longer think of explaining them by utilitarian calculations or by syllogistic reasonings of any sort. He will understand too well the gap that exists between such causes and such effects.

A thing is a force which can be engendered only by another force. In rendering an account of social facts, we seek, then, energies capable of producing them. Not only do the explanations thus given differ from the preceding ones, but they are differently verified, or, rather, it is only with them that the need of verification is felt. If sociological phenomena are only systems of objectivized ideas, to explain them is to rethink them in their logical order, and this explanation is in itself its own proof; at the very most, it will require confirmation by a few examples. Only methodical experiments, on the contrary, can extract from things their real secrets.

If we consider social facts as things, we consider them as social things. The third trait that characterizes our method is that it is exclusively sociological. It has often appeared that these phenomena, because of their extreme complexity, were either inhospitable to science or could be subject to it only when reduced to their elemental conditions, either psychic or organic, that is, only when stripped of their proper nature. We have, on the contrary, undertaken to establish that it is possible to treat them scientifically without removing any of their distinctive characteristics. We have even refused to identify the immateriality of psychological phenomena; we have, furthermore, refused to reabsorb it, with the Italian school, into the general properties of organized matter. We have shown that a social fact can be explained only by another social fact; and at the same time, we have shown how this sort of explanation is possible by pointing out, in the internal social milieu, the principal factor in collective evolution. Sociology is, then, not an auxiliary of any other science; it is itself a distinct and autonomous science, and the feeling of the specificity of social reality is indeed so necessary to the sociologist that only distinctly sociological training can prepare him to grasp social facts intelligently.

In our opinion this progress is the most important that sociology still has to make. No doubt, when a science is in the process of being born, one is obliged, in order to construct it, to refer to the only models that exist, namely, the sciences already formed. These contain a treasure of experiences which it would be foolish to ignore. A science can regard itself as definitely established, however, only when it has achieved independence for itself. For it can justify its existence only when it has for its subject matter an order of facts which the other sciences do not study. It is impossible that the same concepts can fit equally well things of different natures.

Such appear to us to be the principles of sociological method. This collection of rules will perhaps appear needlessly complicated if one compares it with the procedures in current use. All this apparatus of precautions may seem very laborious for a science which, up to this point, scarcely demanded from those who devoted themselves to it more than general and philosophical training. It is certain, indeed, that the practice of such a method cannot have for its effect the popularization of interest in sociological matters. When, as a condition of their acceptance into the sociological fraternity, we ask men to discard the concepts they are accustomed to apply to an order of facts, in order to reexamine the latter in a new way, we cannot expect to recruit a numerous clientele. But this is not the goal toward which we are heading. We believe, on the contrary, that the time has come for sociology to spurn popular success, so to speak, and to assume the exacting character befitting every science. It will then gain in dignity and authority what it will perhaps lose in popularity. For, so long as it remains involved in partisan struggles, is content to expound common ideas with more logic than the layman, and, consequently, presumes no special competence, it has no right to speak loudly enough to silence passions and prejudices. Assuredly, the time when it will be able to play this role successfully is still far off. However, we must begin to work now, in order to put it in condition to fill this role some day.

III SUICIDE

Only two years after the publication of *The Rules of Sociological Method,* Durkheim's *Suicide* appeared. It is the first and one of the greatest of all pieces of sociological research.* The history of research in sociology, in fact, begins with this book, and although its conclusions have been modified in the seventy years since its publication, its importance has suffered no diminishment. The reason for this is not its subject—although suicide has a significant incidence in all societies and ranks therefore as a perennial problem—but rather the sociological lessons it has to teach. What Durkheim has done here is to answer an unissued challenge. That is, if someone reading *The Rules of Sociological Method* in 1895 had said to its author, "Look here, you have told us that social facts are autonomous and that they are independent of psychological facts. You have told us further that any attempt to explain social facts in terms of psychological facts is bound to be false. All this is very well and indeed your arguments are impressive. But where is the evidence? How do you prove it?"

One can imagine Durkheim listening to a challenge of this sort. Indeed, *The Rules* aroused a lively controversy, and Durkheim had himself been forced to take some of the criticisms into account in a preface to the

---

*That is, research in the scientific manner. There had been surveys before, and especially important ones by Le Play in France and Booth in England, but no research in the contemporary sense; that is, research designed to bring evidence to bear for or against a hypothesis, inquiry informed by a theory rather than by an intent to gather facts or acquire information.

second edition. Some of his critics, in a mood of outrage, had indulged in heroic demolitions of points of view he had never entertained, and Durkheim had to insist that some of the views attributed to him had little in common with the views he actually held. He therefore had to reiterate, with all possible care, that he did indeed believe that social facts were things, that they are external to the individual, and that sociology does not—and cannot—rest upon a psychological foundation. But these were still arguments. The proof was lacking. This proof he was to supply in a dramatic fashion in his book on suicide.

What decision could be more intimate and personal than the decision to take one's own life? Suicide, let us remember, is never, by definition, accidental. It is always, on the contrary, premeditated. It is always planned. And it is planned in secret. No one discusses even with his closest friends, much less the members of his family, his preference for suicide as a solution to problems that loom too large. The despondency that precedes suicide is usually accompanied by withdrawal from friends and family, and the potential victim is thrown upon his own resources, which doubtless complicates the problem. Some suicides, it is true, are planned in advance and even sometimes used as a threat in order to improve this or that aspect of a personal relationship, but these—the blackmailing suicides —are the suicides that seldom occur. The suicides that actually happen are premeditated in silence and in secrecy. They are among the most intimate phenomena in human life—even sexual intercourse involves a second person—and they involve the destruction of something that is uniquely one's own.

This, nevertheless, is the phenomenon that Durkheim chooses to show the autonomy of social facts. For however surprising it may seem, a decision to commit suicide, intimate and personal as it is, is a decision that exhibits certain regularities. Its incidence reveals patterns that can be understood only in sociological terms. There is nothing in the individual consciousness that can explain it. It is a social not a psychological fact. It conforms to rules that have nothing to do with individual psychology. This is Durkheim's contention, and this his thesis. It is a remarkable tribute to a remarkable man that he brings it off, and no one since, whatever his minor and modifiable errors, has been able to refute him.

The progress of a science, says Durkheim in his preface to the book, is exhibited by the number of problems it is able to solve. One of the reasons that sociology has not so far appeared in an altogether favorable light is not only the number of problems it has been unable to solve but also the fact that its problems have not so far been clearly defined or clear-cut. Sociology is still unfortunately in the stage of system-building rather than that of problem-solving, and so long as this situation obtains, he implies, sociology cannot take its place among the mature sciences. Too often sociologists have preferred brilliant generalizations to the answers to what have since been called by T. H. Marshall and Robert K. Merton, among others, "problems of the middle range." It is not a vast and imposing philosophy of history that is needed, according to Durkheim, but rather, to use the language of Marshall in his Inaugural Lecture at the University of London many years later, "stepping-stones in the middle distance." It is this middle kind of enterprise that Durkheim's study of suicide represents. Only the enemies of reason could rejoice in the defeat of sociology—what other devices or sciences do we have to solve some of our problems?—and accordingly it is of the greatest importance that our efforts to treat social facts scientifically should meet with success. To this effort the sociologist must himself subscribe and forego those metaphysical reflections and inferior philosophizings that have taken the place of solid sociology in the past. The sociologist must instead "take as the object of his research groups of facts clearly circumscribed, capable of ready definition, with definite limits, and adhere strictly to them."*

Durkheim offers a simple reason that, among so many problems that were available, he chose to study suicide. The study of suicide is timely, of course, but much more important is that few subjects in the social sciences can be more accurately defined and because real laws can be discovered that demonstrate beyond any dialectical argument the genuine possibility of sociology. This does not mean that broader concerns are being neglected. On the contrary, Durkheim believes that he has established a number of propositions about marriage, widowhood, the family, and religion in the course of his research that would be impossible in moralistic or philosophic approaches to these phenomena. He hopes even that he has been able to disclose a number of factors responsible for the general malaise that afflicted European societies at the time of writing.

Finally, the study will exhibit, as nothing else could, the force of the principle in which Durkheim takes so much pride; namely, that social facts have to be studied as things and as realities external to the individual. To agree that social facts are all disclosed in the consciousness of the individual would be to make psychology all-sufficient and to deprive sociology of its subject matter, to give to the latter, as it were, a borrowed existence, and ultimately to deny its possibility. The study of suicide will be able to show, on the contrary, that individuals in society are dominated by a reality that is greater than they, a morality that has its source and origin outside of their individual consciousness, and that is in every sense of the word a collective morality. And it is this collective morality which is a social fact, a fact as

---

*Émile Durkheim, *Suicide: A Study in Sociology*, translated by J. A. Spaulding and George Simpson, and edited with an introduction by George Simpson (Glencoe, Illinois: The Free Press, 1951), p. 36.

definite and as substantial as the facts studied by the other sciences.

Durkheim's procedure as he confronts his task is, first of all, to define his terms. Suicide would seem to have a simple and definite meaning and to present no unusual difficulties for either public consumption or scientific communication. Unfortunately, this is far from the case. Like other words in common use, the concept of suicide is far from being clear and unambiguous. Instead of accepting what seems to be a common usage, the sociologist has to derive his concept inductively, to examine particular instances of its use, and to arrive at some common element in all of these cases. Common usage is in fact much too inexact, and it is therefore necessary to analyze in some detail those actions which should be included within the class of suicides and those which should not. In particular, and this has some importance for later commentators who have wished to attach Durkheim to a particular school of sociological interpretation, an act cannot be defined by the end the actor may say he has in mind, "for an identical system of behavior may be adjustable to too many different ends without altering its nature."* The trouble with the means-end schema is that death may not be the purpose of an action but only an inevitable consequence that is accepted nevertheless, as in the case of a soldier sacrificing himself for his regiment or a mother for her child. The common quality of these facts is that they are undertaken consciously, with knowledge prepense, and with full recognition of the inevitable end. Suicide is therefore to be separated from those actions which have similar conclusions but in which the actor is neither the conscious nor the unconscious author of his own end. The definition at which Durkheim arrives, therefore, is as follows: "The term suicide is applied to all cases of death resulting directly or indirect-

Ibid., p. 43.

ly from a positive or negative act of the victim himself, which he knows will produce this result."* The same act that falls short of actual death is defined as an "attempted suicide."

At the conclusion of his Introduction, Durkheim asks a rhetorical question: Why should the subject of suicide, since it apparently involves an individual's temperament, character, antecedents, and private history, be of any interest to the sociologist at all? Why not leave it to the psychologist? The answer, less rhetorical, is that, when the suicides committed in a given society are taken as a whole, the result is not simply a sum of independent units but a new fact altogether, a fact *sui generis,* a social fact. Indeed, suicide rates for various countries remain at the same level for considerable periods of time, and when they change, the changes can be attributed to fundamental transformations in the societies themselves. At each moment in its history every society has what Durkheim calls its own "aptitude for suicide," and when this is given a quantitative measure, as a proportion of voluntary deaths to all deaths, eleven European countries, for example, present almost the same rank order with respect to one another over a continuing period of time. There is in the suicide rates in fact much more constancy than in the death rates in the same countries.

This, then, is the phenomenon to be explained. Durkheim will proceed by considering, first, the extra-social causes that might be responsible; second, the nature of the social causes that might be involved; and third, the social element in suicide and its relationship to other social facts.

The first extra-social cause of suicide to which Durkheim devotes his attention is psychopathic states, or insanity, and if this can be found in every instance of suicide, in a one-to-one relationship, then it becomes

*Ibid., p. 44.

purely an individual affliction and the problem is solved. Similarly, if suicides are defined as mad and suicide an act of madness, then the psychopathic theory is true by definition. Neither one of these approaches appeals to Durkheim, and indeed he denies that there is such a thing as a suicidal insanity. Certainly the tendency to suicide cannot be a monomania, which it would have to be if the theory were true, because mental flaws cannot be localized. Monomanias, in fact, do not exist; where they seem to appear they are not diseases in and of themselves but secondary manifestations of more serious and more general perturbations. There is no proof that there is a specific monomania that conduces to suicide.

It is still possible, however, that suicides are committed in an insane state and that mental alienation is an inevitable accompaniment. In order to settle this possibility, Durkheim considers four types of suicide that might fit into this category—maniacal suicide, melancholy suicide, obsessive suicide, and impulsive or automatic suicide. In all of these cases, however, the motive is either missing altogether or it is imaginary. Since, in a majority of all suicides, motives are very much to be discerned, it is impossible to explain them all in terms of the motiveless cases and one cannot say therefore that all suicides are insane. Even the melancholia of the insane is different from the dejection of the normal person, both of whom may commit suicide. These reasons seem sufficient to Durkheim to enable him to dismiss insanity as the cause of suicide. All he needs to do is to point to the numerous suicides deliberately undertaken by normal people, people without hallucinations of any sort.

Nor do the statistics support the psychopathic thesis. Insanity has a relatively high incidence among Jews in various countries in comparison with Protestants and Catholics, and at the same time the Jewish suicide rate is very slight. In this situation therefore we find that the suicide rate varies in inverse proportion with the rate of mental illness. The latter, therefore, cannot be the cause of the former. A slight inverse ratio is also observable in a comparison of Protestants and Catholics. Age comparisons of the incidence of mental disease and suicide exhibit a similar absence of relationship. Regional or national comparisons also fail to show correlation; indeed, some countries with the lowest incidence of mental disease have the highest incidence of suicide. There is no consistent agreement, in fact, between the indexes of these two phenomena, no matter what the basis of the comparison. The conclusion that one cannot make a causal connection between suicide and mental disease is therefore clear.

There is one psychopathic state, however, or at least Durkheim so considers it, that requires an additional comment, and that is alcoholism. Alcoholism is a disease to which almost every ill of civilization has been attributed by one writer or another, and suicide is no exception. What can be said for alcoholism as a factor in suicide? The answer is, very little. A look at a wide variety of statistics from different countries and from different regions of the same country shows little or no correlation. An exception is Denmark, where both alcoholism rates and suicide rates are high—and it is necessary to remember that all of these statistics are from Durkheim's own time—but a single case is clearly insufficient to establish a correlation. The northern provinces of France also appear to be an exception, but the relatively higher incidence of alcoholism may be due simply to the rarity of wine and its cost in comparison with other alcoholic liquors. In general there is an inverse relationship between suicide and the drinking of wine, but one may not conclude, on that account, that wine is therefore a specific for the prevention of suicide. All of these conjunctions are fortuitous. The case for alcohol as a factor in suicide, like that of other "mental" or dispositional factors, is one that does not survive examination.

Durkheim follows the same procedure with respect to what he calls "normal psychological states," those having to do with race and heredity. Here again he studies the statistics available to him and concludes in every case that a correlation between the incidence of this or that hereditary factor and suicide is either wholly lacking or, if present, can be explained in some other way, or is fortuitous. One investigator, Morselli for example, had found a correlation between height and suicide among men drafted for military service, but Durkheim is unimpressed, and in this case, as in others, is frequently able to bring contrary statistics to bear. In any event, the notion that there is something hereditary about the tendency to commit suicide is not one to which Durkheim can give any credence.

Geographical factors have also been invoked as explanations of suicide, and it is true that geographical differences sometimes appear. In north temperate regions at the present time, for example, there are more suicides in the merry month of May than in the melancholy month of November. What, then, can be said about the "cosmic environment," the influence of such factors as climate, temperature, latitude, season, the winds (the sirocco for example), the average length of day, the time of day, the days of the week, the rural-urban variable, large cities *vs.* small cities, and so on. In no case can it be proven that geographic or cosmic factors in any way play so important a role that they are directly responsible for the incidence of suicide.

One final theory has to be considered before Durkheim can attend to the social causes of suicide. This factor is the factor of imitation. Since imitation is no longer a sociological concept—nor, for that matter, a psychological one—a word of explanation is in order. One of Durkheim's contemporaries was Gabriel Tarde (1843–1904), for many years a magistrate in the provinces, later director of the division of criminal statistics in the Ministry of Justice in Paris, and finally professor of philosophy in the Collège de France. Tarde had written a number of important books in the fields of criminology and penology and had then turned his attention, too, to sociology. His sociological approach, however, took its departure and continued in a direction different from Durkheim's. Indeed, the directions were diametrically different, and the two writers became opponents in doctrine and in theory. Tarde never tired in his insistence on the importance of psychological factors in the explanations of social interaction and elevated to highest importance in this respect the factor of imitation. In one of his famous statements he had said that, in conforming to custom, we are imitating our ancestors and, in conforming to fashion, we are imitating our contemporaries. Although imitation is not the only process involved in social life—repetition, opposition, and adaptation also play their roles—it is the most important. Needless to say, these views seemed entirely erroneous to Durkheim. Tarde's importance was such, however, that he had to say something about imitation and its possible relationship to suicide. Tarde, incidentally, had a brilliant literary style. If his total impact on the developing science of sociology was less than Durkheim's, one explanation is that Durkheim's views, on the whole, were more cogent. They contributed size to sociology whereas one could derive from Tarde's the implication that sociology is in some sense supererogatory, its problems being at base psychological.

Durkheim's discussion of imitation and its possible role in the commission of suicide is long and complicated, it involves an extended analysis of the meaning of imitation, and it need not detain our attention for more than a minute. He does discover cases of apparent "contagion," where a number of soldiers in the army, patients in hospitals, and inmates of prisons committed suicide in quick succession. He is even willing to admit that something can be said for the theory of contagion. A detailed examination of the incidence of suicide in France in ecological terms, however, fails to disclose centers of concentration from which such contagion has spread. The maps of incidence will show a relatively even distribution with no central nucleus and consequently they indicate nothing with respect to the factor of imitation. That there may be imitation in individual cases, Durkheim does not deny. But they do not affect the suicide rate in general. Organs of public opinion, and especially newspapers, may stimulate the thought of suicide, but they rarely if ever motivate the act. Durkheim, finally, cannot resist the temptation to remark how weak the theory of imitation is in general as an explanation of any of the phenomena of collective life.

These preliminaries disposed of, Durkheim is ready to turn more positively to an examination of the social causes of suicide. One of the problems associated with the study of this phenomenon in the past has been that there was no adequate classification, either with respect to motives or with respect to other characteristics. Statistics of this kind are extraordinarily difficult to compile and it seems preferable, therefore, to proceed in terms of cause rather than of characteristics in an endeavor to discover if different types of suicide exist. Furthermore, "the nature of a phenomenon is much more profoundly got at by knowing its cause than by knowing its characteristics only, even the essential ones."*

It is necessary in this connection, however, to be exceedingly cautious about the reasons that are ordinarily assigned to suicide (such reasons, for example, as poverty, family troubles, jealousy, and so on), because these may be only apparent causes. Statistical efforts should not be invoked in order to solve these "insoluble problems of moral casuistry"; on the contrary, much more can be expected from a study of the social con-

Ibid., p. 147.

comitants of suicide, which are, of course, also susceptible to statistical treatment. By social concomitants Durkheim means such things as religion, marital status, political preference, occupational affiliation, and so on.

How then, to take the first of these, does religion
affect the suicide rate? An examination of the data reveals a consistent pattern. Roman Catholic countries
have the lowest suicide rates, mixed Protestant and
Catholic countries next and Protestant countries the highest. Greek Orthodox countries have even lower rates than
the Roman Catholic, but differences in culture may out-
weigh differences in religion and it would be hazardous,
therefore, to draw an inference. The Catholic and Protestant rates, however, are taken from comparable cultures,
although differences between Spain and Portugal on the
one hand, and Germany on the other, are still large
enough to make a possible difference. When figures for
Germany alone are taken, however, the correlation continues—the Bavarians, who are preponderately Catholic, have lower rates than the Prussians, who are preponderately Protestant. The case of Switzerland is strik-
ingly clear; the Protestant cantons show four to five
times as many suicides as do the Catholic cantons. In
every place where statistics are available, in fact, Protestants show far more suicides than Catholics. The "aptitude" of the Jews for suicide is most frequently less
even than that of Catholics, although this relationship is
sometimes reversed, as in Bavaria.

It is difficult to explain the Protestant-Catholic
difference in terms of doctrine. Both religions forbid suicide and they do so with equal emphasis. Indeed, in
strict doctrinal terms there is no difference between
them. The explanation almost has to lie therefore in the
fact that Protestantism gives greater freedom to inquiry
than Catholicism does and that, in the latter, one is required to submit without intellectual scrutiny to the
dogmas of faith. In Protestantism traditional beliefs
have been overthrown and tradition itself plays a much

more modest role. But it is not the free thought itself that causes the difference; this, indeed, is one of the results of something more fundamental, and that is the rise of sectarianism that accompanies the overthrow of traditional beliefs. Free inquiry derives from schisms and presupposes them; it also stimulates and multiplies them. As this process continues, more and more is left to individual judgment and less and less to an authoritarian, comprehensive, and controlling creed. As a result Protestantism in general is much less integrated in its social organization than is Catholicism, and the bonds that tie the individual member to the group are much less binding. The individual is therefore thrown more and more upon his own resources and lacks a corporate group to whom to appeal when he feels the need for stability and support. There is a close correlation also between free inquiry and the love of learning, and wherever the latter is in evidence—in the upper classes as opposed to the lower, the educated as opposed to the uneducated, and men in comparison with women— there also the suicide rates are higher. The fact that the Jews are learned and also disinclined to suicide would seem to contradict the hypothesis until it is remembered that anti-Semitism has given them an extraordinary sense of cohesion.

Men do not, however, kill themselves because of their learning or their desire to pursue the truth in freedom. They do so because of the disorganization that goes along with the lack of cohesion in a body of the faithful. To this conclusion Durkheim appends an eloquent statement in defense of science—"Let those who view anxiously and sadly the ruins of ancient beliefs, who feel all the difficulties of these critical times, not ascribe to science an evil it has not caused but rather which it tries to cure!"* Freedom of inquiry does, it must be admitted, conduce to suicide, but only because

Ibid., p. 169.

of the dissolution of old traditions and ancient sentiments that no longer have vitality. On the other hand, religion has a "prophylactic" effect on suicide, not because of its doctrinal proscription of the act but because it is practiced by a group and because this group in turn supports the sentiments of an integrated and collective life. It is the cohesion of the religious community, most clearly in Catholicism, that tends to preserve the individual life and to protect it from suicide.

If it is the social organization of a religion or, as Durkheim calls it, a religious society, that deters men from taking their own life, what can be said about another kind of society, namely the domestic society? One would be inclined to think that the unmarried, having fewer responsibilities, would also have fewer suicides. Exactly the reverse, however, turns out to be the case. The rate of the married is everywhere lower than that of the unmarried. The rates for those who have been married and who have lost their spouses through death vary somewhere in between those for the married and the unmarried, and this varies from society to society as to which of the two sexes is more favored. "Facts being thus determined," says Durkheim, "let us seek explanations."*

Two causes may be invoked to explain the relative immunity of the married—either the apparently soothing influence of the domestic environment or the prior and positive factor of marital selection. The latter means that persons who marry are already more favored than those who do not in qualities of health, wealth, and morality, and are therefore in a category less disposed to begin with to suicide. Durkheim's statistics, however, force him for a number of reasons to regard this explanation with scepticism and to turn his attention instead to the first of the factors, the influence of the family itself.

Ibid., p. 180.

The family, however, may mean two different things, and the following passage indicates as clearly as anything in the entire corpus the penetrating quality of Durkheim's mind:

> For the family environment consists of different elements. For husband and wife alike the family includes: 1. the wife or husband; 2. the children. Is the salutary effect of the family on the suicidal tendency due to the former or the latter? In other words, the family consists of two different associations: the conjugal group and the family group proper. These two societies have not the same origin, nor the same nature, nor consequently, in all probability, the same effects. One springs from a contract and elective affinity, the other from a natural phenomenon, consanguinity; the former unites two members of the same generation, the latter unites one generation to the next; the latter is as old as humanity, the former was organized at a relatively late date. Since they are here so different it is not *a priori* certain that both combine equally to produce the fact we are studying. Anyway, if both contribute to it this cannot be in the same manner, nor probably in the same measure. Thus, we must investigate whether both take part and, if so, the share of each.*

Thus in these few words Durkheim recognizes with a piercing and altogether French clarity that the family has two aspects and is indeed two different kinds of groups—the conjugal on the one hand and the consanguine on the other—and that these two groups might possibly exert different affects upon the incidence of suicide. This distinction, of course, is now taken for granted, but some kind of genius is required to make it with the kind of clarity and precision that Durkheim brings to it for the first time.

*Ibid., p. 185.

It is not marriage that influences the suicide rate. From the beginning of the nineteenth century to the time of Durkheim's writing, the marriage rate changed very little whereas the suicide rate increased threefold. Similarly, countries with comparable marriage rates disclose suicide rates that differ by wide margins. Furthermore, the suicide rate among childless married men is only a little lower than the suicide rate among unmarried men. Nothing could be clearer then that neither marriage itself, nor the conjugal family, is the significant causal factor in suicide. The limited influence of marriage is also suggested by the fact that the rate for widowers with children is less than that of married men without them. And finally, the rate for childless wives is very considerably higher than that for unmarried women. The conclusion at which Durkheim arrives, therefore, is that "the immunity of married persons in general is thus due, wholly for one sex [the male] and largely for the other [the female], to the influence not of conjugal society but of the family society."*

The story of suicide is thus one that has something to do with the degree of integration of the group. One measure of integration, of course, is the number and intensity of the interactions that occur and the number of collective sentiments that appear. If this is true of the family, it is no less true of political societies and this, without following his argument in detail, Durkheim is also able to show with reference to a number of separate countries in different stages of their growth and development. Although the statistics are not so reliable, and certainly not so complete, as he would like to have them, Durkheim shows that the facts he can adduce are susceptible to only one interpretation in order to explain the diminished rate of suicide in time of political turmoil, revolution, and war:

*Ibid., p. 189.

Great social disturbances and great popular wars rouse collective sentiments, stimulate partisan spirit and patriotism, political and national faith, alike, and concentrating activity toward a single end, at least temporarily cause a stronger integration of society. The salutary influence which we have just shown to exist is due not to the crisis but to the struggles it occasions. As they force men to close ranks and confront the common danger, the individual thinks less of himself and more of the common cause. Besides, it is comprehensible that this integration may not be purely momentary but may sometimes outlive its immediate causes, especially when it is intense.*

Thus, once more, we have an illustration from Durkheim of the sociological principle now expressed in more modern language, that any threat on the part of an out-group intensifies the cohesion of the in-group. And anything that contributes to the cohesion of a group will have the supplementary effect of reducing the rate of suicide.

Durkheim in this way arrives at this proposition: Suicide varies inversely with the degree of integration of a religious group, a domestic group, or a political group. It is not the religion itself, in the first instance, that has the moderating effect, nor the domestic and political arrangements in the second and third; but rather the degree of integration that the group exhibits. The general conclusion thus follows that "suicide varies inversely with the degree of integration of the social groups of which the individual forms a part."†

This conclusion, however important, explains only one type of suicide, the type that Durkheim calls "egoistic." There are other kinds as well, for which other explanations have to be sought. The second kind of sui-

*Ibid., p. 208.
†Ibid., p. 209.

cide, to which he now turns his attention, is the "altruistic."

For, inconsistent as it may seem, if insufficient integration increases the suicide rate, so also does excessive integration. In the first case there is too much individuality and in the second too little; and both produce the same result. It often happens, in primitive as well as other societies, that suicide becomes a duty, an obligation, a satisfaction of a social demand or a religious requirement, and in these circumstances men tend to commit it precisely because they recognize their obligation to the group. Thus, the Danish warriors who considered it a disgrace to die in bed, the Japanese who observe the custom of hara-kiri, the men of ancient Ceos who, heads crowned with flowers, drank the hemlock together in solemn ceremony. Similarly, although Durkheim does not use this example, the Prussian officer who, upon his conviction by a court-martial, is ritualistically given his own pistol and who knows without question what to do with it. And similarly also the Hindu widow who succumbs in the rite of suttee. All these are cases of persons who commit suicide because it is their duty to do so. It is a duty they recognize and accept for the reason that they are members of a highly cohesive social group.

We thus confront a type of suicide differing by incisive qualities from the preceding one. Whereas the latter is due to excessive individuation, the former is caused by too rudimentary individuation. One occurs because society allows the individual to escape it, being insufficiently aggregated in some parts or even in the whole; the other, because society holds him in too strict tutelage. Having given the name of *egoism* to the state of the ego living its own life and obeying itself alone, that of *altruism* adequately expresses the opposite state, where the ego is not its own property, where it is blended with something not itself, where the goal of conduct is exterior to itself, that is, in one of the groups in which it participates. So we call the suicide caused by intense altruism *altruistic suicide*.*

This type of suicide, however, is not always obligatory. Sometimes it is optional in the sense that society does not demand it of the individual but rather creates the conditions under which it is desirable. So long as prestige is attached to it, whether or not the obligatory character obtains, it remains a form of altruistic suicide. Martyrdom is perhaps as good an illustration of this phenomenon as any that can be found, and here again the act is praiseworthy. Altruistic suicide appears quite frequently in the more primitive societies, but it is by no means absent from the more civilized, and especially certain kinds of groups in the latter, including religious associations and elite military corps—all of which is wholly consistent with the theory. The degree of integration that an individual has with his group, therefore, can have two contrary effects with respect to suicide, but this is only because two different types of suicide are involved, the egoistic on the one hand and the altruistic on the other. Some writers, it is true, including some of Durkheim's followers, prefer to call the latter "sacrifice" rather than "suicide." But however one solves the semantic issue, the thesis retains its cogency.

There is still a third type of suicide, and this is the *anomic*. This type has to do neither with too much integration nor too little, but is a result rather of the crises of societies. Among these crises are, of course, economic crises and political crises, the former resulting from sudden changes in the economic conditions of the country, symbolized for example by a crash on the market. With regard to the former, it cannot be emphasized too strongly that it is not poverty *per se* that conduces to suicide but rather sudden changes in the economic situations of people. Poverty itself, as the case of Ireland

Ibid., p. 221.

shows, is almost a protection against the temptation to commit suicide. Prosperity also has a kind of insulating effect. It is rather rapid changes in the economic equilibrium—economic disturbances—that exert a positive influence upon the suicide rate.

Durkheim introduces the word "anomy" almost casually and explains the type of suicide for which it is a label as follows:

> Anomy, therefore, is a regular and specific factor in suicide in our modern societies; one of the springs from which the annual contingent feeds. So we have here a new type to distinguish from the others. It differs from them in its dependence, not on the way in which individuals are attached to society, but on how it regulates them. Egoistic suicide results from man's no longer finding a basis for existence in life; altruistic suicide, because this basis for existence appears to man situated beyond life itself. The third sort of suicide, the existence of which has just been shown, results from man's activity's lacking regulation and his consequent sufferings. By virtue of its origin we shall assign this last variety the name of *anomic suicide.**

If egoistic and altruistic suicide are paired contraries, so also does anomic suicide have a contrary and this Durkheim calls "fatalistic suicide." Anomic suicide occurs in a time of societal turbulence when the norms disappear and no longer function therefore as instruments of social control. Fatalistic suicide, on the contrary, is a phenomenon of too much control, of a societal restraint that tends to be oppressive and constant and therefore, apparently, unbearable. Although cases are difficult to find, it may be illustrated by the very young married man, the childless married woman, and the slave. Durkheim himself accords it little importance and indeed

Ibid., p. 258.

treats it only in a footnote.

One of the many interesting features of Durkheim's study of suicide is that, in spite of his emphasis on the social causes and conditions of this universal phenomenon, he nevertheless allows himself to speculate on the individual victim as he contemplates the act of self-destruction. One cannot say that the author here renounces his own thesis. On the contrary, he is more concerned to show that the suicides that come into his ken can indeed be categorized as one or another of his three major types. The chapter in which he discusses the individual forms of these types also indicates that sometimes the act represents a combination of types.

In the penultimate chapter of his book, Durkheim tilts with both Quetelet and Tarde. He finds little difficulty in disposing of the former's theory of the average man, or average type, or average anything else as any explanation of any social phenomenon. The suicide, after all, is far from typical; even in countries where suicide appears with the greatest frequency, the rate is only three or four hundred in every million inhabitants. Quetelet's notion that some kind of stability can be accounted for either by averages or by majorities therefore ignores altogether the fact that phenomena that appear only in small minorities also exhibit stability and regularity. Exceptions to the general rule also have their invariabilities. For these propositions the suicide rates in various countries provide ample proof.

Tarde, on the contrary, emphasized the importance of imitation, itself an individual and therefore a psychological process. He wrote indeed, as quoted by Durkheim,* that "anything social, whether a word of a language, a religious rite, an artisan's skill, an artistic method, a legal statute or a moral maxim is transmitted and passes from an individual parent, teacher, friend, neighbor, or

*Ibid., p. 308.

comrade to another individual." Durkheim is willing to concede that some ideas and sentiments pass in this way from one generation to the next and that this explanation may be considered satisfactory "as a last resort." However, it is wholly incapable of explaining the phenomenon of suicide. Are we to suppose, he asks, in a rare display of sarcasm, that everyone who commits suicide had as his teacher the year before someone who committed suicide and that he in turn will communicate, transmit, and pass on to another individual this same propensity? The question shows how false and ridiculous it is to try to account for a social phenomenon like suicide in terms of individual or interindividual phenomena. There is not a single fact, in short, that can lend cogency to Tarde's view of the transmission of social phenomena in general. In suicide there is no filiation—no affiliation and no apparentation. The explanation has to be sought on an impersonal or social level that transcends the existence of individual cases.

This chapter, entitled "The Social Element of Suicide," rises to such heights of eloquence that we shall reprint it as a whole in the sequel. It is in this place, above all, that Durkheim insists that collective tendencies have an existence of their own, that they are as real as cosmic forces, and that as social facts they affect the individual from without. They are things of their own kind and they are objective. The thesis thus advanced in the earlier book on method thus receives an overwhelming support from the facts of the moral life and especially from the statistics of suicide.

Durkheim is not so naive, of course, as to suppose that his thesis will be easily accepted, especially since it seems to imply that there is some greater or more important reality to be attached to collective sentiments and tendencies than to individual sentiments and tendencies. He is nevertheless disposed to defend it with vigor and ingenuity on the ground that new facts—social facts—do emerge from the association of other, individual facts, that the whole is somehow more than the sum of its parts, and that there is such a thing as the emergence of novel phenomena the characteristics and qualities of which cannot be predicted from a knowledge of the elements composing them.

These views, however, proved to be serious obstacles in the general acceptance of and reaction to Durkheim's general sociological theory. American sociologists were especially resistant to them on the ground that Durkheim seemed quite clearly in these words to be hypostatizing abstractions, to be making "things," as it were, out of words, to be violating the law of parsimony—sacred to scientific method—in creating entities beyond necessity, and to be declaring that society is somehow more "real" than the individuals who compose it. Long suspicious of German metaphysics and nurtured instead on an empirical and nominalistic tradition, the Americans viewed this approach with disfavor and demanded to know in what the "reality" of society consists if not in individuals. They were similarly suspicious, and for the same reasons, of any independent entity called a "collective consciousness," an entity with its own reality and, as Durkheim insisted, *external* to individuals.

It must probably be conceded, on this point, that Durkheim was guilty of a certain extravagance in his language and that another choice of words would have forestalled some of the criticisms and obviated some of the difficulties. It was in fact unnecessary for him to raise metaphysical issues at all and clearly unwise to raise them in so challenging a manner without at the same time trying to meet and solve them on their own ground—i.e., the ground on which philosophers had been arguing about them for centuries. If he had been content to defend the objectivity of social facts, for example, and had ignored the question of their "reality," he would have silenced at least the outcries of the metaphysicians without sacrificing the core of his doctrine, which was, of course, the insistence on a range of phenomena sufficiently different from others to justify the independent existence of the science of sociology. From these observations we can learn the lesson that the language in which a theory is couched is often as important as the theory itself and that sometimes the former has unfortunate consequences for the latter. The point, in short, is that, if Durkheim had espoused the same thesis without using either the word "reality" or the concept of "collective conscience," it would have attracted few of the strictures that it did in fact encounter.

The importance of the thesis, however, cannot be gainsaid. Durkheim has shown with elegance and power that there is something in society, in the collective life as it were, that exerts an influence on individuals and indeed makes them what they come to be. There are social facts that impose external restraints upon individuals and operate too as positive guides to action. If one thinks, for example, of the dependence of individuals upon the arrangement of material things—arrangements with which he has had nothing personally to do —then the significance becomes clear. The buildings that we inhabit and use, the streets and the roads and the rails over which we drive our vehicles, the house furnishings and clothing that we have—all these and more (what would be called the "material culture" in the contemporary texts) antedate a particular use by a particular individual. They are *there,* so to speak, ready for him, and to them, as external facts, he must adjust his actions. But if these material things exercise constraint and guidance, it is no less true that nonmaterial things can have the same effect. We adjust not only to the vehicles of transportation but also to its schedules, not only to the architecture of our churches but also to the rituals and dogmas of belief, not only to the playing fields but also to the rules of the games we play upon them, not only to our national monuments but to the creeds and heroic deeds that they memorialize, and not only to the letters of the alphabet but to the meanings that words convey. All of these are external to the individual. All of them are social facts. And they all testify to the existence of a realm of phenomena that belongs specifically and uniquely to sociology.

This in essence is the import and significance of Durkheim's great work on suicide. It is important not for what it tells us about the processes of self-destruction, although this is a subject of perennial interest and one to the substantive understanding of which Durkheim made a major contribution, but far more for what it tells us about the nature of man and society. Suicide is a significant and ever-present phenomenon in all human societies. Its causes and changing rates under different circumstances require constant study, investigation, and research. We shall always need to know more about it. Once we have said all this, however, and even emphasized it, it remains true that Durkheim's work is not only a study of suicide; it is also a study of ourselves and of the societies in which we live. If it were only about suicide, it would maintain first rank as a study of that phenomenon. But it is also about man and society and the relations between them, and so it achieves major rank in addition as one of the classic works in the history of sociology. Once again, in concluding our discussion of this book, we may say that its dramatic significance lies in the incontrovertible evidence that Durkheim gives us that even so intimate and personal a matter as the decision to commit suicide cannot possibly be understood in psychological terms or by any reference to individual victims. Suicide—even suicide—is a social phenomenon.

We reprint now Durkheim's chapter entitled "The Social Element of Suicide," which contains in essence most of his principal theses.

The Social Element of Suicide*

Now that we know the factors in terms of which the social suicide-rate varies, we may define the reality to which this rate corresponds and which it expresses numerically.

I The individual conditions on which suicide might, *a priori,* be supposed to depend, are of two sorts.

There is first the external situation of the agent. Sometimes men who kill themselves have had family sorrow or disappointments to their pride, sometimes they have had to suffer poverty or sickness, at others they have had some moral fault with which to reproach themselves, etc. But we have seen that these individual peculiarities could not explain the social suicide-rate; for the latter varies in considerable proportions, whereas the different combinations of circumstances which consititute the immediate antecedents of individual cases of suicide retain approximately the same relative frequency. They are therefore not the determining causes of the act which they precede. Their occasionally important role in the premeditation of suicide is no proof of being a causal one. Human deliberations, in fact, so far as reflective consciousness affects them are often only purely formal, with no object but confirmation of a resolve previously formed for reasons unknown to consciousness.

Besides, the circumstances are almost infinite in number which are supposed to cause suicide because they rather frequently accompany it. One man kills

Ibid., pp. 297–325.

himself in the midst of affluence, another in the lap of poverty; one was unhappy in his home, and another had just ended by divorce a marriage which was making him unhappy. In one case a soldier ends his life after having been punished for an offense he did not commit; in another, a criminal whose crime has remained unpunished kills himself. The most varied and even the most contradictory events of life may equally serve as pretexts for suicide. This suggests that none of them is the specific cause. Could we perhaps at least ascribe causality to those qualities known to be common to all? But are there any such? At best one might say that they usually consist of disappointments, of sorrows, without any possibility of deciding how intense the grief must be to have such tragic significance. Of no disappointment in life, no matter how insignificant, can we say in advance that it could not possibly make existence intolerable; and, on the other hand, there is none which must necessarily have this effect. We see some men resist horrible misfortune, while others kill themselves after slight troubles. Moreover, we have shown that those who suffer most are not those who kill themselves most. Rather it is too great comfort which turns a man against himself. Life is most readily renounced at the time and among the classes where it is least harsh. At least, if it really sometimes occurs that the victim's personal situation is the effective cause of his resolve, such cases are very rare indeed and accordingly cannot explain the social suicide-rate.

Accordingly, even those who have ascribed most influence to individual conditions have sought these conditions less in such external incidents than in the intrinsic nature of the person, that is, his biological constitution and the physical concomitants on which it depends. Thus, suicide has been represented as the product of a certain temperament, an episode of neurasthenia, subject to the effects of the same factors as neurasthenia. Yet we have found no immediate and regular relationshp between neurasthenia and the social suicide-rate. The two facts even vary at times in inverse proportion to one another, one being at its minimum just when and where the other is at its height. We have not found, either, any definite relation between the variations of suicide and the conditions of physical environment supposed to have most effect on the nervous system, such as race, climate, temperature. Obviously, though the neuropath may show some inclination to suicide under certain conditions, he is not necessarily destined to kill himself; and the influence of cosmic factors is not enough to determine in just this sense the very general tendencies of his nature.

Wholly different are the results we obtained when we forgot the individual and sought the causes of the suicidal aptitude of each society in the nature of the societies themselves. The relations of suicide to certain states of social environment are as direct and constant as its relations to facts of biological and physical character were seen to be uncertain and ambiguous. Here at last we are face to face with real laws, allowing us to attempt a methodical classification of types of suicide. The sociological causes thus determined by us have even explained these various concurrences often attributed to the influence of material causes, and in which a proof of this influence has been sought. If women kill themselves much less often than men, it is because they are much less involved than men in collective existence; thus they feel its influence—good or evil —less strongly. So it is with old persons and children, though for other reasons. Finally if suicide increases from January to June but then decreases, it is because social activity shows similar seasonal fluctuations. It is therefore natural that the different effects of social activity should be subject to an identical rhythm, and consequently be more pronounced during the former of these two periods. Suicide is one of them.

The conclusion from all these facts is that the social suicide-rate can be explained only sociologically. At any given moment the moral constitution of society establishes the contingent of voluntary deaths. There is, therefore, for each people a collective force of a definite amount of energy, impelling men to self-destruction. The victim's acts which at first seem to express only his personal temperament are really the supplement and prolongation of a social condition which they express externally.

This answers the question posed at the beginning of this work. It is not mere metaphor to say of each human society that it has a greater or lesser aptitude for suicide; the expression is based on the nature of things. Each social group really has a collective inclination for the act, quite its own, and the source of all individual inclination, rather than their result. It is made up of the currents of egoism, altruism or anomy running through the society under consideration with the tendencies to languorous melancholy, active renunciation, or exasperated weariness derivative from these currents. These tendencies of the whole social body, by affecting individuals, cause them to commit suicide. The private experiences usually thought to be the proximate causes of suicide have only the influence borrowed from the victim's moral predisposition, itself an echo of the moral state of society. To explain his detachment from life the individual accuses his most immediately surrounding circumstances; life is sad to him because he is sad. Of course his sadness comes to him from without in one sense, however not from one or another incident of his career but rather from the group to which he belongs. This is why there is nothing which cannot serve as an occasion for suicide. It all depends on the intensity with which suicidogenetic causes have affected the individual.

II Besides, the stability of the social suicide-rate would itself sufficiently show the truth of this conclusion. Though we have, for methodological reasons, delayed the problem until now, it will nevertheless admit of no other solution.

When Quetelet drew to the attention of philosophers the remarkable regularity with which certain social phenomena repeat themselves during identical periods of time, he thought he could account for it by his theory of the average man—a theory, moreover, which has remained the only systematic explanation of this remarkable fact. According to him, there is a definite type in each society more or less exactly reproduced by the majority, from which only the minority tends to deviate under the influence of disturbing causes. For example, there is a sum total of physical and moral characteristics represented by the majority of Frenchmen and not found in the same manner or degree among the Italians or the Germans, and vice versa. As these characteristics are by definition much the most widespread, the actions deriving from them are also much the most numerous; these constitute the great groups. Those, on the contrary, determined by divergent qualities are relatively rare, like these qualities themselves. Again, though not absolutely unchangeable, this general type varies much more slowly than an individual type; for it is much more difficult for a society to change en masse than for one or a few individuals, singly, to do so. This stability naturally recurs in the acts derived from the characteristic attributes of this type; the former remain the same in quantity and quality so long as the latter do not change, and as these same ways of behaviour are also the commonest, stability must necessarily be the general law of those manifestations of human activity described by statistics. The statistician, in fact, takes into account all events of an identical nature which occur within a given society. Therefore, since most of them remain invariable so long as the general type of the society is unchanged, and since, on the other hand, its changes are unusual, the results of statistical enumerations must necessarily remain the same for fairly long series of consecutive years. Facts derived from special qualities and individual occurrences are not, to be sure, subject to the same regularity; therefore, stability is never absolute. But they are the exception; this is why invariability is the rule, while change is exceptional.

Quetelet gave the name *average type* to this general type, because it is obtained almost exactly by taking the arithmetic means of the individual types. If, for example, after having determined the height of all persons in a given social group, one adds them and divides by the number of individuals measured the result arrived at expresses with quite sufficient accuracy the most common height. For the differences of greater or less, the giants and dwarfs, probably are about equal in number. Thus they offset each other, annul each other mutually and accordingly have no effect on the quotient.

The theory seems very simple. But first, it can only be considered as an explanation if it shows how the average type is realized in the great majority of individuals. For the average type to remain constantly equal to itself while they change, it must be to some extent independent of them; and yet it must also have some way of insinuating itself into them. Of course, the question ceases to be significant if the average type is admitted to be the same as the ethnic type. For the constituent elements of the race, having their origin outside the individual, are not subject to the same variations as he; and yet they are realized only in him. They can thus well be supposed to penetrate the truly individual elements and even act as their base. Only, for this explanation to apply to suicide, the tendency impelling a man to kill himself must depend strictly on race; but we know that the facts contradict this hypothesis. Shall we suppose that the general condition of the social environment, being the same for most individuals, affects nearly all in the same way and so partially bestows a common appearance on them? But the social environment is fundamentally one of common ideas, beliefs, customs and tendencies. For them to impart themselves thus to individuals, they must somehow exist independently of individuals; and this approaches the solution we suggested. For thus is implicitly acknowledged the existence of a collective inclination to suicide from which individual inclinations are derived, and our whole problem is to know of what it consists and how it acts.

But there are still other considerations. However the preponderance of the average man is explained, this conception could never account for the regularity of the reproduction of the social suicide-rate. Actually, by definition, the only possible characteristics this type involves are those found in the major part of the population. But suicide is the act of a minority. In the countries where it is most common, 300 or 400 cases per million inhabitants at most are found. It is radically excluded by the average man's instinct of self-preservation; the average man does not kill himself. But in that case, if the inclination to self-destruction is rare and anomalous, it is wholly foreign to the average type and so, even a profound knowledge of the latter could not even explain the source of suicides, still less help us understand the stability of the number of suicides in a given society. In short, Quetelet's theory rests on an inaccurate observation. He thought it certain that stability occurs only in the most general manifestations of human activity; but it is equally found in the sporadic manifestations which occur only at rare and isolated points of the social field. He thought he had met all the requirments by showing how, as a last resort, one could explain the invariability of what is not exceptional; but the exception itself has its own invariability, inferior to none. Everyone dies; every living organism is so made up that it cannot escape dissolution. There are, on the contrary, very few people who kill themselves; the great majority of men have no inclination to suicide. Yet the suicide-rate is even more stable than that of general mortality. The close connection which Quetelet sees between the commonness of a quality and its permanence therefore does not exist.

Besides, the result to which his own method leads confirms this conclusion. By this principle, in order to calculate the intensity of any quality belonging to the average type, one must divide the sum of the items displaying this quality within the society under consideration by the number of individuals capable of producing them. Thus, in a country like France, where for a long time there have not been more than 150 suicides per million inhabitants, the average intensity of the suicidal inclination would be expressed by the proportion 150/1,000,000 or 0.00015; and in England, where there are only 80 cases for an equal number, this proportion would be only 0.00008. There would therefore be an inclination to suicide, of this strength, in the average individual. But such figures practically amount to zero. So weak an inclination is so far from an act that it may be considered non-existent. It has not strength enough to occasion a single suicide unaided. It is not, therefore, the commonness of such an inclination which can explain why so many suicides are committed annually in one or the other of these two societies.

Even this estimate is infinitely exaggerated. Quetelet reached it only by arbitrarily ascribing a certain affinity for suicide to men on the average, and by estimating the strength of this affinity according to manifestations not observed in the average man, but only among a small number of exceptional persons. Thus, the abnormal was used to determine the normal. To be sure, Quetelet thought to escape this objection by noting that abnormal cases, which occur sometimes in one and sometimes in the other direction, mutually compensate and offset each other. But such compensation occurs only for qualities which are found in varying degrees in everybody, such as height. We may in fact assume that unusually tall and unusually short persons are about numerically equal to each other. The average of these exceptional heights may therefore practically be equal to the most usual height: so that only the latter appears at the end of the total calculation. The contrary actually takes place in regard to a naturally exceptional fact, such as the suicidal inclination. In this case Quetelet's procedure can only artificially introduce into the average type an element which falls outside the average. To be sure, as we have just seen, it occurs there only in a very dilute state, precisely because the number of individuals among whom it is distributed is far greater than it should be. But if the mistake is of little practical importance, it none the less exists.

In reality, the meaning of the relation calculated by Quetelet is simply the probability that a single man belonging to a definite social group will kill himself during the year. If there are 15 suicides annually in a population of 100,000 souls, we may well conclude that there are 15 chances in 100,000 that some person will commit suicide during this same unit of time. But this probability in no sense gives us a measure of the average inclination to suicide, or helps prove the existence of such an inclination. The fact that so many individuals out of 100 kill themselves does not imply that the others are exposed to any degree and can teach us nothing concerning the nature and intensity of the causes leading to suicide.

Thus the theory of the average man does not solve the problem. Let us take the problem up again, then, and see how it presents itself. Victims of suicide are in an infinite minority, which is widely dispersed; each one of them performs his act separately, without knowing that others are doing the same; and yet, so long as society remains unchanged the number of suicides remains the same. Therefore, all these individual manifestations, however independent of one another they seem, must surely actually result from a single cause or a single group of causes, which dominate individuals. Otherwise how could we explain that all these individual wills, ignorant of one another's existence, annually achieve the same end in the same numbers? At least for the most part they have no effect upon one another; they are in no way conjoined; yet everything takes place as if they were obeying a single order. There must then be some force in their common environment inclining them all in the same direction, whose greater or lesser strength causes the greater or lesser number of individual suicides. Now the effects revealing this force vary not according to organic and cosmic environments but solely according to the state of the social environment. This force must then be collective. In other words, each people has collectively an inclination of its own to suicide, on which the size of its contribution to voluntary death depends.

From this point of view there is no longer anything mysterious about the stability of the suicide-rate, any more than about its individual manifestations. For since each society has its own temperament, unchangeable within brief periods, and since this inclination to suicide has its source in the moral constitution of groups, it must differ from group to group and in each of them remain for long periods practically the same. It is one of the essential elements of social coenaesthesia. Now this coenaesthetic state, among collective existences as well as among individuals, is their most personal and unchangeable quality, because nothing is more fundamental. But then the effects springing from it must have both the same personality and the same stability. It is even natural for them to possess a higher stability than that of general mortality. For temperature, climatic and geological influences, in a word the various conditions on which public health depends, change much more readily from year to year than the temperament of peoples.

There is however another hypothesis, apparently different from the above, which might be tempting to some minds. To solve the difficulty, might we not suppose that the various incidents of private life considered to be preeminently the causes determining suicide, regularly recur annually in the same proportions? Let us suppose that every year there are roughly the same number of unhappy marriages, bankruptcies, disappointed ambitions, cases of poverty, etc. Numerically the same and analogously situated, individuals would then naturally form the resolve suggested by their situation, in the same numbers. One need not assume that they yield to a superior influence; but merely that they reason generally in the same way when confronted by the same circumstances.

But we know that these individual events, though preceding suicides with fair regularity, are not their real causes. To repeat, no unhappiness in life necessarily causes a man to kill himself unless he is otherwise so inclined. The regularity of possible recurrence of these various circumstances thus cannot explain the regularity of suicide. Whatever influence is ascribed to them, moreover, such a solution would at best change the problem without solving it. For it remains to be understood why these desperate situations are identically repeated annually, pursuant to a law peculiar to each country. How does it happen that a given, supposedly stable society always has the same number of disunited families, of economic catastrophes, etc.? This regular recurrence of identical events in proportions constant within the same population but very inconstant from one population to another would be inexplicable had not each society definite currents impelling its inhabitants with a definite force to commercial and industrial ventures, to behaviour of every sort likely to involve families in trouble, etc. This is to return under a very slightly different form to the same hypothesis which had been thought refuted.

III   Let us make an effort to grasp the meaning and import of the terms just employed.

Usually when collective tendencies or passions are spoken of, we tend to regard expressions as mere metaphors and manners of speech with no real signification but a sort of average among a certain number of individual states. They are not considered as things, forces *sui generis* which dominate the consciousness of single individuals. None the less this is their nature, as is brilliantly shown by statistics of suicide. The individuals making up a society change from year to year, yet the number of suicides is the same so long as the society itself does not change. The population of Paris renews itself very rapidly; yet the share of Paris in the total of French suicides remains practically the same. Although only a few years suffice to change completely the personnel of the army, the rate of military suicides varies only very slowly in a given nation. In all countries the evolution of collective life follows a given rhythm throughout the year; it grows from January to about July and then diminishes. Thus, though the members of the several European societies spring from widely different average types, the seasonal and even monthly variations of suicide take place in accordance with the same law. Likewise, regardless of the diversity of individual temperaments, the relation between the aptitude for suicide of married persons and that of widowers and widows is identically the same in widely differing social groups, from the simple fact that the moral condition of widowhood everywhere bears the same relation to the moral constitution characteristic of marriage. The causes which thus fix the contingent of voluntary deaths for a given society or one part of it must then be independent of individuals, since they retain the same intensity no matter what particular persons they operate on. One would think that an unchanging manner of life would produce unchanging effects. This is true; but a way of life is something, and its unchanging character requires explanation. If a way of life is unchanged while changes occur constantly among those who practise it, it cannot derive its entire reality from them.

It has been thought that this conclusion might be avoided through the observation that this very continuity was the work of individuals and that, consequently, to account for it there was no need to ascribe to social phenomena a sort of transcendency in relation to individual life. Actually, it has been said, "anything social, whether a word of a language, a religious rite, an artisan's skill, an artistic method, a legal statute or a moral maxim is transmitted and passes from an individual parent, teacher, friend, neighbor, or comrade to another individual."

Doubtless if we had only to explain the general way in which an idea or sentiment passes from one generation to another, how it is that the memory of it is not lost, this explanation might as a last resort be considered satisfactory. But the transmission of facts such as suicide and, more broadly speaking, such as the various acts reported by moral statistics, has a very special nature not to be so readily accounted for. It relates, in fact, not merely in general to a certain way of acting, but to the number of cases in which this way of acting is employed. Not merely are there suicides every year, but there are as a general rule as many each year as in the year preceding. The state of mind which causes men to kill themselves is not purely and simply transmitted, but—something much more remarkable—transmitted to an equal number of persons, all in such situations as to make the state of mind become an act. How can this be if only individuals are concerned? The number as such cannot be directly transmitted. Today's population has not learned from yesterday's the size of the contribution it must make to suicide; nevertheless, it will make one of identical size with that of the past, unless circumstances change.

Are we then to imagine that, in some way, each suicide had as his initiator and teacher one of the victims of the year before and that he is something like his moral heir? Only thus can one conceive the possibility that the social suicide-rate is perpetuated by way of interindividual traditions. For if the total figure cannot be transmitted as a whole, the units composing it must be transmitted singly. According to this idea, each suicide would have received his tendency from some one of his predecessors and each act of suicide would be something like the echo of a preceding one. But not a fact exists to permit the assumption of such a personal filiation between each of these moral occurrences statistically registered this year, for example, and a similar event of the year before. As has been shown above, it is quite exceptional for an act to be inspired in this way by another of like nature. Besides, why should these ricochets occur regularly from year to year? Why should the generating act require a year to produce its counterpart? Finally, why should it inspire a single copy only? For surely each model must be reproduced only once on the average, or the total would not be constant. Such an hypothesis, as arbitrary as it is difficult to conceive, we need discuss no longer. But if it is dropped, if the numerical equality of annual contingents does not result from each particular case producing its counterpart in the ensuing period, it can only be due to the permanent action of some impersonal cause which transcends all individual cases.

The terms therefore must be strictly understood. Collective tendencies have an existence of their own; they are forces as real as cosmic forces, though of another sort; they, likewise, affect the individual from without, though through other channels. The proof that the reality of collective tendencies is no less than that of cosmic forces is that this reality is demonstrated in the same way, by the uniformity of effects. When we find that the number of deaths varies little from year to year, we explain this regularity by saying that mortality depends on the climate, the temperature, the nature of the soil, in brief on a certain number of material forces which remain constant through changing generations because independent of individuals. Since, therefore, moral acts such as suicide are reproduced not merely with an equal but with a greater uniformity, we must likewise admit that they depend on forces external to individuals. Only, since these forces must be of a moral order and since, except for individual men, there is no other moral order of existence in the world but society, they must be social. But whatever they are called, the important thing is to recognize their reality and conceive of them as a totality of forces which cause us to act from without, like the physicochemical forces to which we react. So truly are they things *sui generis* and not mere verbal entities that they may be measured, their relative sizes compared, as is done with the intensity of electric currents or luminous foci. Thus, the basic proposition that social facts are objective, a proposition we have had the opportunity to prove in another work and which we consider the fundamental principle of the sociological method, finds a new and especially conclusive proof in moral statistics and above all in the statistics of suicide. Of course, it offends common sense. But science has encountered incredulity whenever it has revealed to men the existence of a force that has been overlooked. Since the system of accepted ideas must be modified to make room for the new order of things and to establish new concepts, men's minds resist through mere inertia. Yet this understanding must be reached. If there is such a science as sociology, it can only be the study of a world hitherto unknown, different from those explored by the other sciences. This world is nothing if not a system of realities.

But just because it encounters traditional prejudices this conception has aroused objections to which we must reply.

First, it implies that collective tendencies and

thoughts are of a different nature from individual tendencies and thoughts, that the former have characteristics which the latter lack. How can this be, it is objected, since there are only individuals in society? But, reasoning thus, we should have to say that there is nothing more in animate nature than inorganic matter, since the cell is made exclusively of inanimate atoms. To be sure, it is likewise true that society has no other active forces than individuals; but individuals by combining form a psychical existence of a new species, which consequently has its own manner of thinking and feeling. Of course the elementary qualities of which the social fact consists are present in germ in individual minds. But the social fact emerges from them only when they have been transformed by association since it is only then that it appears. Association itself is also an active factor productive of special effects. In itself it is therefore something new. When the consciousness of individuals, instead of remaining isolated, becomes grouped and combined, something in the world has been altered. Naturally this change produces others, this novelty engenders other novelties, phenomena appear whose characteristic qualities are not found in the elements composing them.

This proposition could only be opposed by agreeing that a whole is qualitatively identical with the sum of its parts, that an effect is qualitatively reducible to the sum of its productive causes; which amounts to denying all change or to making it inexplicable. Someone has, however, gone so far as to sustain this extreme thesis, but only two truly extraordinary reasons have been found for its defense. First, it has been said that "in sociology we have through a rare privilege intimate knowledge both of that element which is our individual consciousness and of the compound which is the sum of consciousness in individuals"; secondly, that through this twofold introspection "we clearly ascertain that if the individual is subtracted nothing remains of the social."

The first assertion is a bold denial of all contemporary psychology. Today it is generally recognized that psychical life, far from being directly cognizable, has on the contrary profound depths inaccessible to ordinary perception, to which we attain only gradually by devious and complicated paths like those employed by the sciences of the external world. The nature of consciousness is therefore far from lacking in mystery for the future. The second proposition is purely arbitrary. The author may of course state that in his personal opinion nothing real exists in society but what is individual, but proofs supporting this statement are lacking and discussion is therefore impossible. It would be only too easy to oppose to this the contrary feeling of a great many persons, who conceive of society not as the form spontaneously assumed by individual nature, on expanding outwardly, but as an antagonistic force restricting individual natures and resisted by them! What a remarkable intuition it is, by the way, that lets us know directly and without intermediary both the element—the individual—and the compound, society? If we had really only to open our eyes and take a good look to perceive at once the laws of the social world, sociology would be useless or, at least very simple. Unfortunately, facts show only too clearly the incompetence of consciousness in this matter. Never would consciousness have dreamt, of its own accord, of the necessity which annually reproduces demographic phenomena in equal numbers, had it not received a suggestion from without. Still less can it discover their causes, if left to its own devices.

But by separating social from individual life in this manner, we do not mean that there is nothing psychical about the former. On the contrary, it is clear that essentially social life is made up of representations. Only these collective representations are of quite another character from those of the individual. We see no objection to calling sociology a variety of psychology, if we

carefully add that social psychology has its own laws
which are not those of individual psychology. An example will make the thought perfectly clear. Usually the
origin of religion is ascribed to feelings of fear or rever-
ence inspired in conscious persons by mysterious and
dreaded beings; from this point of view, religion seems
merely like the development of individual states of mind
and private feelings. But this over-simplified explanation
has no relation to facts. It is enough to note that the institution of religion is unknown to the animal kingdom,
where social life is always very rudimentary, that it is
never found except where a collective organization exists,
that it varies with the nature of societies, in order to conclude justifiably that exclusively men in groups think
along religious lines. The individual would never have
risen to the conception of forces which so immeasurably
surpass him and all his surroundings, had he known nothing but himself and the physical universe. Not even the
great natural forces to which he has relations could have
suggested such a notion to him; for he was originally
far from having his present knowledge of the extent of
their dominance; on the contrary, he then believed that
he could control them under certain conditions. Science
taught him how much he was their inferior. The power
thus imposed on his respect and become the object of
his adoration in society, of which the gods were only
the hypostatic form. Religion is in a word the system of
symbols by means of which society becomes conscious
of itself; it is the characteristic way of thinking of collective existence. Here then is a great group of states of
mind which would not have originated if individual
states of consciousness had not combined, and which
result from this union and are superadded to those which
derive from individual natures. In spite of the minutest
possible analysis of the latter, they will never serve to
explain the foundation and development of the strange
beliefs and practices from which sprang totemism, the
origin of naturism from it and how naturism itself be-

came on the one hand the abstract religion of Jahweh, on the other, the polytheism of the Greeks and Romans, etc. All we mean by affirming the distinction between the social and the individual is that the above observations apply not only to religion, but to law, morals, customs, political institutions, pedagogical practices, etc., in a word to all forms of collective life.

Another objection has been made, at first glance apparently more serious. Not only have we admitted that the social states of mind are qualitatively different from individual ones, but that they are in a sense exterior to individuals. We have not even hesitated to compare this quality of being external with that of physical forces. But, it is objected, since there is nothing in society except individuals, how could there be anything external to them?

If the objection were well founded we should face an antinomy. For we must not lose sight of what has been proved already. Since the handful of people who kill themselves annually do not form a natural group, and are not in communication with one another, the stable number of suicides can only be due to the influence of a common cause which dominates and survives the individual persons involved. The force uniting the conglomerate multitude of individual cases, scattered over the face of the earth, must necessarily be external to each of them. If it were really impossible for it to be so, the problem would be insoluble. But the impossibility is only apparent.

First, it is not true that society is made up only of individuals; it also includes material things, which play an essential role in the common life. The social fact is sometimes so far materialized as to become an element of the external world. For instance, a definite type of architecture is a social phenomenon; but it is partially embodied in houses and buildings of all sorts which, once constructed, become autonomous realities, independent of individuals. It is the same with the avenues of communication and transportation, with instruments and machines used in industry or private life which express the state of technology at any moment in history, of written language, etc. Social life, which is thus crystallized, as it were, and fixed on material supports, is by just so much externalized, and acts upon us from without. Avenues of communication which have been constructed before our time give a definite direction to our activities, depending on whether they connect us with one or another country. A child's taste is formed as he comes into contact with the monuments of national taste bequeathed by previous generations. At times such monuments even disappear and are forgotten for centuries, then, one day when the nations which reared them are long since extinct, reappear and begin a new existence in the midst of new societies. This is the character of those very social phenomena called Renaissances. A Renaissance is a portion of social life which, after being so to speak, deposited in material things and remained long latent there, suddenly reawakens and alters the intellectual and moral orientation of peoples who had had no share in its construction. Doubtless it could not be reanimated if living centers of consciousness did not exist to receive its influence; but these individual conscious centers would have thought and felt quite differently if this influence were not present.

The same remark applies to the definite formulae into which the dogmas of faith are precipitated, or legal precepts when they become fixed externally in a consecrated form. However well digested, they would of course remain dead letters if there were no one to conceive their significance and put them into practice. But though they are not self-sufficient, they are none the less in their own way facts of social activity. They have a manner of action of their own. Juridical relations are widely different depending on whether or not the law is written. Where there is a constituted code, jurisprudence is more regular but less flexible, legislation more uniform but also more rigid. Legislation adapts itself less readily to a variety of individual cases, and resists innovations more strongly. The material forms it assumes are thus not merely ineffective verbal combinations but active realities, since they produce effects which would not occur without their existence. They are not only external to individual consciousness, but this very externality establishes their specific qualities. Because these forms are less at the disposal of individuals, individuals cannot readily adjust them to circumstances, and this very situation makes them more resistant to change.

Of course it is true that not all social consciousness achieves such externalization and materialization. Not all the aesthetic spirit of a nation is embodied in the works it inspires; not all of morality is formulated in clear precepts. The greater part is diffused. There is a large collective life which is at liberty; all sorts of currents come, go, circulate everywhere, cross and mingle in a thousand different ways, and just because they are constantly mobile are never crystallized in an objective form. Today, a breath of sadness and discouragement descends on society; tomorrow, one of joyous confidence will uplift all hearts. For a while the whole group is swayed towards individualism; a new period begins and social and philanthropic aims become paramount. Yesterday cosmopolitanism was the rage, today patriotism has the floor. And all these eddies, all these fluxes and refluxes occur without a single modification of the main legal and moral precepts, immobilized in their sacrosanct forms. Besides, these very precepts merely express a whole sub-jacent life of which they partake; they spring from it but do not supplant it. Beneath all these maxims are actual, living sentiments, summed up by these formulae but only as in a superficial envelope. The formulae would awake no echo if they did not correspond to definite emotions and impressions scattered through society. If, then, we ascribe a kind of reality to them, we do not dream of supposing them to be the whole of moral reality. That would be to take the sign for the thing signified. A sign is certainly something; it is not a kind of supererogatory epiphenomenon; its role in intellectual development is known today. But after all it is only a sign.

But because this part of collective life has not enough consistency to become fixed, it none the less has the same character as the formulated precepts of which we were just speaking. It is external to each average individual taken singly. Suppose some great public danger arouses a gust of patriotic feeling. A collective impulse follows, by virtue of which society as a whole assumes axiomatically that private interests, even those usually regarded most highly, must be wholly effaced before the common interest. And the principle is not merely uttered as an ideal; if need be it is literally applied. Meanwhile, take a careful look at the average body of individuals. Among very many of them you will recapture something of this moral state of mind, though infinitely attenuated. The men who are ready to make freely so complete a self-abnegation are rare, even in time of war. Therefore there is not one of all the single centers of consciousness who make up the great body of the nation, to whom the collective current is not almost wholly exterior, since each contains only a spark of it.

The same thing is observable in respect to even the stablest, most fundamental moral sentiments. Every society, for example, has a respect for the life of man in general, the intensity of which is determined by and commensurate with the relative weight of the penalties attached to homicide. The average man, on the other hand, certainly feels something of the same sort, but far less and in a quite different way from society. To appreciate this difference, we need only compare the emotion one may individually feel at sight of the murderer or even of the murder, and that which seizes assembled crowds under the same circumstances. We know how far they may be carried if unchecked. It is because, in this case, anger is collective. The same difference constantly appears between the manner in which society resents these crimes and the way in which they affect individuals; that is, between the individual and the social form of the sentiment offended. Social indignation is so strong that it is very often satisfied only by supreme expiation. The private person, however, provided that the victim is unknown or of no interest to him, that the criminal does not live near and thus constitute a personal threat to him, though thinking it proper for the crime to be punished, is not strongly enough stirred to feel a real need for vengeance. He will not take a step to discover the guilty one; he will even hesitate to give him up. Only when public opinion is aroused, as the saying goes, does the matter take on a different aspect. Then we become more active and demanding. But it is opinion speaking through us; we act under the pressure of the collectivity, not as individuals.

Indeed, the distance between the social state and its individual repercussions is usually even greater. In the above case, the collective sentiment, in becoming individualized, retained, at least among most people, strength enough to resist acts by which it is offended; horror at the shedding of human blood is sufficiently deeply enrooted in most consciences today to prevent the outburst of homicidal thoughts. But mere misappropriation, quiet, non-violent fraud, are far from inspiring us with equal aversion. Not many have enough respect for another's rights to stifle in the germ every wish to enrich themselves fraudulently. Not that education does not develop a certain distaste for all unjust actions. But what a difference between this vague, hesitant feeling, ever ready for compromise, and the categorical, unreserved and open stigma with which society punishes theft in all shapes! And what of so many other duties still less rooted in the ordinary man, such as the one that bids us contribute our just share to public expense, not to defraud the public treasury, not to try to avoid military service, to execute contracts faithfully, etc.? If morality in all these respects were only guaranteed by the uncertain feelings of the average conscience, it would be extremely unprotected.

So it is a profound mistake to confuse the collective type of a society, as is so often done, with the average type of its individual members. The morality of the average man is of only moderate intensity. He possesses only the most indispensable ethical principles to any decided degree, and even they are far from being as precise and authoritative as in the collective type, that is, in society as a whole. This, which is the very mistake committed by Quetelet, makes the origin of morality an insoluble problem. For since the individual is in general not outstanding, how has a morality so far surpassing him succeeded in establishing itself, if it expresses only the average of individual temperaments? Barring a miracle, the greater cannot arise from the lesser. If the common conscience is nothing but the most general conscience, it cannot rise above the vulgar level. But then whence come the lofty, clearly imperative precepts which society undertakes to teach its children, and respect for which it enforces upon its members? With good reason, religions and many philosophies with them have regarded morality as deriving its total reality only from God. For the pallid, inadequate sketch of it contained in individual consciences cannot be regarded as the original type. This sketch seems rather the result of a crude, unfaithful reproduction, the model for which must therefore exist somewhere outside individuals. This is why the popular imagination, with its customary over-simplicity, assigns it to God. Science certainly could waste no time over this conception, of which it does not even take cognizance. Only, without it no alternative exists but to leave morality hanging unexplained in the air or make it a system of collective states of conscience. Morality either springs from nothing given in the world of experience, or it springs from society. It can only exist in a conscience; therefore, if it is not in the individual conscience it is in that of the group. But then it must be admitted that the latter, far from being confused with the average conscience, everywhere surpasses it.

Observation thus confirms our hypothesis. The regularity of statistical data, on the one hand, implies the existence of collective tendencies exterior to the individual, and on the other, we can directly establish this exterior character in a considerable number of important cases. Besides, this exteriority is not in the least surprising for anyone who knows the difference between the individual and social states of consciousness. By definition, indeed, the latter can reach none of us except from without, since they do not flow from our personal predispositions. Since they consist of elements foreign to us they express something other than ourselves. To be sure in so far as we are solidary with the group and share its life, we are exposed to their influence; but so far as we have a distinct personality of our own we rebel against and try to escape them. Since everyone leads this sort of double existence simultaneously, each of us has a double impulse. We are drawn in a social direction and tend to follow the inclinations of our own natures. So the rest of society weighs upon us as a restraint to our centrifugal tendencies, and we for our part share in this weight upon others for the purpose of neutralizing theirs. We ourselves undergo the pressure we help to exert upon others. Two antagonistic forces confront each other. One, the collective force, tries to take possession of the individual; the other, the individual force, repulses it. To be sure, the former is much stronger than the latter, since it is made of a combination of all the individual forces; but as it also encounters as many resistances as there are separate persons, it is partially exhausted in these multifarious contests and reaches us disfigured and enfeebled. When it is very strong, when the circumstances activating it are of frequent recurrence, it may still leave a deep impression on individuals; it arouses in them mental states of some vivacity which, once formed, function with the spontaneity of instinct; this happens in the case of the most essential moral ideas. But most social currents are either too weak or too intermittently in contact with us to strike deep roots in us; their action is superficial. Consequently, they remain almost completely external. Hence, the proper way to measure any element of a collective type is not to measure its magnitude within individual consciences and to take the average of them all. Rather, it is their sum that must be taken. Even this method of evaluation would be much below reality, for this would give us only the social sentiment reduced by all its losses through individuation.

So there is some superficiality about attacking our conception as scholasticism and reproaching it for assigning to social phenomena a foundation in some vital principle or other of a new sort. We refuse to accept that these phenomena have as a substratum the conscience of the individual, we assign them another; that formed by all the individual consciences in union and combination. There is nothing substantival or ontological about this substratum, since it is merely a whole composed of parts. But it is just as real nevertheless, as the elements that make it up; for they are constituted in this very way. They are compounds, too. It is known today that the ego is the resultant of a multitude of conscious states outside the ego; that each of these elementary states, in turn, is the product of unconscious vital units, just as each vital unit is itself due to an association of inanimate particles. Therefore if the psychologist and the biologist correctly regard the phenomena of their study as well founded, merely through the fact of their connection with a combination of elements of the next lower order, why should it not be the same in sociology? Only those have the right to consider such a basis inadequate who have not renounced the hypothesis of a vital force and of a substantive soul. Nothing is more reasonable, then, than this proposition at which such offense has been taken; that a belief or social practice may exist independently of its individual expressions. We clearly did not imply by this that society can exist without individuals, an obvious absurdity we might have been spared having attributed to us. But we did mean: 1. that the group formed by associated individuals has a reality of a different sort from each individual considered singly; 2. that collective states exist in the group from whose nature they spring, before they affect the individual as such and establish in him in a new form a purely inner existence.

Such a way of considering the individual's relations to society also recalls the idea assigned the individual's relations with the species or the race by contemporary zoologists. The very simple theory has been increasingly abandoned that the species is only an individual perpetuated chronologically and generalized spatially. Indeed it conflicts with the fact that the variations produced in a single instance become specific only in very rare and possibly doubtful cases. The distinctive characteristics of the race change in the individual only as they change in the race in general. The latter has therefore some reality whence come the various shapes it assumes among individual beings, far from its consisting simply of a generalization of these beings. We naturally cannot regard these doctrines as finally demonstrated. But it is enough for us to show that our sociological conceptions, without being borrowed from another order of research, are indeed not without analogies to the most positive sciences.

IV   Let us apply these ideas to the question of suicide; the solution we gave at the beginning of this chapter will become more precise if we do so.

No moral idea exists which does not combine in proportions varying with the society involved, egoism, altruism and a certain anomy. For social life assumes both that the individual has a certain personality, that he is ready to surrender it if the community requires, and finally, that he is to a certain degree sensitive to ideas of progress. This is why there is no people among whom these three currents of opinion do not co-exist, bending men's inclinations in three different and even opposing directions. Where they offset one another, the moral agent is in a state of equilibrium which shelters him against any thought of suicide. But let one of them exceed a certain strength to the detriment of the others, and as it becomes individualized, it also becomes suicidogenetic, for the reasons assigned.

Of course, the stronger it is, the more agents it contaminates deeply enough to influence them to suicide, and inversely. But this very strength can depend only on the three following sorts of causes: 1. the nature of the individuals composing the society; 2. the manner of their association, that is, the nature of the social organization; 3. the transitory occurrences which disturb the functioning of the collective life without changing its anatomical constitution, such as national crises, economic crises, etc. As for the individual qualities, they can play a role only if they exist in all persons. For strictly personal ones or those of only small minorities are lost in the mass of the others; besides, from their differences from one another they neutralize one another and are mutually eradicated during the elaboration resulting in the collective phenomenon. Only general human characteristics, accordingly, can have any effect. Now these are practically immutable; at least, their change would require more centuries than the life of one nation can occupy. So the social conditions on which the number of suicides depends are the only ones in terms of which it can vary; for they are the only variable conditions. This is why the number of suicides remains stable as long as society does not change. This stability does not exist because the state of mind which generates suicide is found through some chance in a definite number of individuals who transmit it, for no recognizable reason, to an equal number who will imitate the act. It exists because the impersonal causes which gave it birth and which sustain it are the same. It is because nothing has occurred to modify either the grouping of the social units or the nature of their concurrence. The actions and reactions interchanged among them therefore remain the same; and so the ideas and feelings springing from them cannot vary.

To be sure, it is very rare, if not impossible, for one of these currents to succeed in exerting such preponderant influence over all points of the society. It always reaches this degree of energy in the midst of restricted surroundings containing conditions specially favorable to its development. One or another social condition, occupation, or religious faith stimulates it more especially. This explains suicide's twofold character. When considered in its outer manifestations, it seems as though these were just a series of disconnected events; for it occurs at separated places without visible interrelations. Yet the sum of all these individual cases has its own unity and its own individuality, since the social suicide-rate is a distinctive trait of each collective personality. That is, though these particular environments where suicide occurs most frequently are separate from one another dispersed in thousands of ways over the entire territory, they are nevertheless closely related; for they are parts of a single whole, organs of a single organism, as it were. The condition in which each is found therefore depends on the general condition of society. There is a close solidarity between the virulence achieved by one or another of its tendencies and the intensity of the tendency in the whole social body. Altruism is more or less a force in the army depending on its role among the civilian population, intellectual individualism is more developed and richer in suicides in Protestant environments the more pronounced it is in the rest of the nation, etc. Everything is tied together.

But though there is no individual state except insanity which may be considered a determining factor of suicide, it seems certain that no collective sentiment can affect individuals when they are absolutely indisposed to it. The above explanation might be thought inadequate for this reason, until we have shown how the currents giving rise to suicide find at the very moment and in the very environments in which they develop a sufficient number of persons accessible to their influence.

If we suppose, however, that this conjunction is really always necessary and that a collective tendency cannot impose itself by brute force on individuals with no preliminary predisposition, then this harmony must be automatically achieved; for the causes determining the social currents affect individuals simultaneously and predispose them to receive the collective influence. Between these two sorts of factors there is a natural affinity, from the very fact that they are dependent on, and expressive of the same cause: this makes them combine and become mutually adapted. The hypercivilization which breeds the anomic tendency and the egoistic tendency also refines nervous systems, making them excessively delicate; through this very fact they are less capable of firm attachment to a definite object, more impatient of any sort of discipline, more accessible both to violent irritation and to exaggerated depression. Inversely, the crude, rough culture implicit in the excessive altruism of primitive man develops a lack of sensitivity which favors renunciation. In short, just as society largely forms the individual, it forms him to the same extent in its own image. Society, therefore, cannot lack the material for its needs, for it has, so to speak, kneaded it with its own hands.

The role of individual factors in the origin of suicide

can now be more precisely put. If, in a given moral environment, for example, in the same religious faith or in the same body of troops or in the same occupation, certain individuals are affected and certain others not, this is undoubtedly, in great part, because the former's mental constitution, as elaborated by nature and events, offers less resistance to the suicidogenetic current. But though these conditions may share in determining the particular persons in whom this current becomes embodied, neither the special qualities nor the intensity of the current depend on these conditions. A given number of suicides is not found annually in a social group just because it contains a given number of neuropathic persons. Neuropathic conditions only cause the suicides to succumb with greater readiness to the current. Whence comes the great difference between the clinician's point of view and the sociologist's. The former confronts exclusively particular cases, isolated from one another. He establishes, very often, that the victim was either nervous or an alcoholic, and explains the act by one or the other of these psychopathic states. In a sense he is right; for if this person rather than his neighbors committed suicide, it is frequently for this reason. But in a general sense this motive does not cause people to kill themselves, nor, especially, cause a definite number to kill themselves in each society in a definite period of time. The productive cause of the phenomenon naturally escapes the observer of individuals only; for it lies outside individuals. To discover it, one must raise his point of view above individual suicide and perceive what gives them unity. It will be objected that if enough neurasthenics did not exist, social causes would not produce all their effects. But no society exists in which the various forms of nervous degeneration do not provide suicide with more than the necessary number of candidates. Only certain ones are called, if this manner of speech is permitted. These are the ones who through circumstances have been nearer the pessimistic currents and who consequently have felt their influence more completely.

But a final question remains. Since each year has an equal number of suicides, the current does not strike simultaneously all those within its reach. The persons it will attack next year already exist; already, also, most of them are enmeshed in the collective life and therefore come under its influence. Why are they provisionally spared? It may indeed be understood why a year is needed to produce the current's full action; for since the conditions of social activity are not the same according to season, the current too changes in both intensity and direction at different times of the year. Only after the annual cycle is complete have all the combinations of circumstances occurred, in terms of which it tends to vary. But since, by hypothesis, the next year only repeats the last and causes the same combinations, why was not the first enough? Why, to use the familiar expression, does society pay its bill only in installments?

What we think explains this delay is the way time affects the suicidal tendency. It is an auxiliary but important factor in it. Indeed, we know that the tendency grows incessantly from youth to maturity, and that it is often ten times as great at the close of life as at its beginning. The collective force impelling men to kill themselves therefore only gradually penetrates them. All things being equal they become more accessible to it as they become older, probably because repeated experiences are needed to reveal the complete emptiness of an egoistic life or the total vanity of limitless ambition. Thus, victims of suicide complete their destiny only in successive layers of generations.

IV THE ELEMENTARY FORMS OF THE RELIGIOUS LIFE

As in *Suicide* so in this, the last of his four major works, Durkheim is interested in the phenomenon he is investigating not for its own sake but for the light it can shed upon the nature of man. Thus, in *The Elementary Forms of the Religious Life,* Durkheim sets out to study one of the most primitive religions known to mankind. He does this, however, not because of any antiquarian curiosity and not because of an intrinsic interest in simple societies as such, but rather—and this has been the dominant theme throughout his career—because of what they tell us about the larger issues of man and society, and of man in society. This is the paint, he seems to say, that we need to spread upon the canvas, and it must be obvious that we are interested not so much in the paint itself, colorful as it may be, as in the picture that will emerge.

We have previously indicated that Durkheim maintained an agnostic position with respect to religion from his early youth throughout his life. It may seem strange, therefore, to find him devoting a long book to this subject. It might even seem as if, in his comparisons of the religious beliefs of the more primitive societies with those of the more sophisticated, he is mounting a subtle attack upon the latter. This, however, is not his design. Indeed, whatever his personal credo might be, no sociologist can fail to be impressed by the fact that religion is a human institution and that all human institutions have basic supports in the societies in which they arise. "The most barbarous and the most fantastic rites and the strangest myths translate some human need, some aspect of life, either individual or social. The reasons with which the faithful justify them may be, and generally are, erroneous; but the true reasons do not cease to exist, and it is the duty of science to discover them."* To discover these reasons, then, is one of the principal purposes of Durkheim's inquiry.

The study of religion is important for yet another reason. It sheds light not only upon what men believe but, more fundamentally, on what and how they think. The importance of religion far transcends the nature of religion itself. It reaches to the nature of human knowledge. It is a formative factor in the development—one might even say the construction—of the human intellect. For if we will but think, we shall note that, at the root of all of our ideas, of all of our notions and our knowledge, there lie certain ultimate principles, which philosophers since Aristotle have called "categories," which give order and arrangement to our perceptions and sensations, and which thus enable us to know. It is a simple epistemological fact that, although they are indispensable avenues to knowledge, perceptions and sensations do not themselves constitute knowledge and need therefore to be tied together and fastened down to something more stable and universal. The things to which they are thus fastened are the most basic ideas of all, and include the categories of time, space, cause, number, substance, and form. Like the who, what, when, where, and how of the journalist, these categories serve the scientist and the philosopher, indeed every man of knowledge, to give both form and substance (themselves categories, which we cannot avoid) to the succession of sensations with which we are beneficently afflicted. What, then, is the origin of these categories? How do they come to be? The answer—and here Durkheim anticipates one of his principal theses—is that

*Emile Durkheim, *The Elementary Forms of the Religious Life,* translated by J. W. Swain (N.Y.: Collier Books, 1961), pp. 14–15.

they are products of religion. In this way Durkheim intends to solve one of the central problems of the sociology of knowledge.

So fascinated is he by this possibility that he attacks the problem in depth even before finishing his Introduction. Indeed, he proceeds to find fault with the two orthodox, yet contradictory, answers given it in the history of philosophy—one the answer of empiricism and the other the answer of *apriorism,* or, perhaps, to use a less awkward word, Kantianism (although Durkheim makes no reference here to Kant). In the former view, the categories arise wholly from our experience, coming to us as impressions or sensations from the external world and, after establishment, in turn impressing themselves upon the sensations that continue to come to us in experience. Since all sensations are individual and different, however, it is difficult in terms of this theory to explain how men in general come to have and to operate with the same categories, how, in short, an uncommon and idiosyncratic world could become a common and nomothetic one. Spencer's theory that what might be called the "inheritance of acquired categories" could explain this common character is useless for the purpose, if indeed it is not erroneous. For it is clear that a hereditary accumulation could add nothing—no common patterns, for example—that was not first in the experience of the concrete individuals themselves. As a matter of fact, to attempt to derive the categories from experience is to deprive them of two essential properties, their universality and their necessity, and for all of these reasons the answer of empiricism must be wrong. It is not only wrong, says Durkheim; it is also irrational, and this, to a Frenchman, is a killing indictment.

The theory of *apriorism*—that is, that the categories exist somehow in the human mind as prior conditions of experience and without which experience would be meaningless and chaotic—receives rather higher marks from Durkheim, but it does not finally satisfy him. The apriorists, of course, are the rationalists and they believe (reasonably enough) both that the world has a logical order and that reason is able to express this order. They have to believe in addition, however, that the mind transcends experience to the extent of its capacity to arrange and in fact "to know" the sensations of experience, and for this transcendence they can offer no adequate explanation. Certainly it is no explanation to say that this is the nature of the intellect itself, as Leibnitz, for example, had been moved to say in response to Locke. As a matter of fact the rationalists here confront a mystery they are unable to solve. Avoiding the difficulties of the empiricists, they nevertheless founder on difficulties of their own, difficulties that are no less serious and no less insoluble. Finally, if the categories are innately a part of the human intellect they would seem to be in addition immutable, and it is the attainment of immutability that dooms them. For nothing human is immutable.

Let us not despair. If there is an eternal debate between the rationalists and the empiricists on this question, it is only because the arguments on both sides have an equivalent cogency. Neither can therefore conquer, and the question of the origin of the categories remains. Fortunately, however, there is a superior answer, one supplied by the new science of sociology, one that escapes the difficulties of both of the traditional answers, and one that offers a new attitude, a new approach, and new hope. It is ridiculously easy to see—as Durkheim almost seems to imply—that the categories of the understanding have their origin in society, that they are social in source and substance. The categories are "essentially"—and this is Durkheim's word—collective representations; they depend upon the mental state of the group and reflect the manner in which the group is organized and deployed. They are in fact *col-*

lective representations, not individual representations, and one can no more derive the former from the latter than one can "deduce society from the individual, the whole from the part, the complex from the simple."

For society, as Durkheim again asserts and insists, is a reality of its own kind:

> Society is a reality *sui generis;* it has its own peculiar characteristics, which are not found elsewhere and which are not met with again in the same form in all the rest of the universe. The representations which express it have a wholly different content from purely individual ones and we may rest assured in advance that the first add something to the second.
>
> Even the manner in which the two are formed results in differentiating them. Collective representations are the result of an immense co-operation, which stretches out not only into space but into time as well; to make them, a multitude of minds have associated, united and combined their ideas and sentiments; for them, long generations have accumulated their experience and their knowledge. A special intellectual activity is therefore concentrated in them which is infinitely richer and complexer than that of the individual. From that one can understand how the reason has been able to go beyond the limits of empirical knowledge. It does not owe this to any vague mysterious virtue but simply to the fact that according to the well-known formula, man is double. There are two beings in him: an individual being which has its foundation in the organism and the circle of whose activities is therefore strictly limited, and a social being which represents the highest reality in the intellectual and moral order that we can know by observation—I mean society. This duality of our nature has as its consequence in the practical order, the irreducibility of a moral idea to a utilitarian motive, and in the order of thought, the irreducibility of reason to

individual experience. In so far as he belongs to society, the individual transcends himself, both when he thinks and when he acts.*

In this brilliant and forceful passage Durkheim accomplishes several things. In the first place he offers a solution to the problem of knowledge, one that will make forever unnecessary the quarrels of rationalist and empiricist; for the answer in both cases has a partial quality that the sociological view can supplement and to which it can contribute totality. Sociology thus answers what has hitherto been an insoluble epistemological problem. In the second place, he tells us that the ideas we entertain have their source in a long tradition and that they are the product of many minds and many generations as they recede in time. In the third place he is emphasizing once more his conviction that society is a reality of its own kind and can thus serve as the subject of its own science—namely, the science of sociology.

Durkheim's virtues are clear in this passage but so also, unfortunately, are some of his difficulties. The ontological status of collective representations continues to create a problem, and those who followed such philosophies as pragmatism and naturalism could not easily be wooed by notions that smack of an objective idealism, albeit one of a new sociological variety. The notion of "transcendence," which Durkheim employs in this passage, was enough to arouse suspicion.

Nor can it be contended that Durkheim's argument, however attractive it may seem, has succeeded in solving the epistemological problem. He offers a new and ingenious theory of the origin of the categories of the understanding, but he does not seem to notice that he has created problems of a new and different kind. By locating the categories in society he has made of them, so to speak, social facts, facts characterized by exteriority and constraint and, as such, facts that are objec-

*Ibid., pp. 28–29.

tive and external. His problem then is to explain how they become internal, how they come to be part of the apparatus of the mind as it orders the sensations and perceptions that flow into it. The categories may be collective representations, and therefore social, but it is still necessary to explain how they become so integral part of the mind and play there so important and necessary a role in our knowledge of the external world.

Whatever the difficulty, however, it must be conceded that Durkheim makes a major assault on two of the most imposing problems in Western thought—the origin of religion and the origin of knowledge. One can hardly pay him a high enough compliment for the sustained brilliance with which he attacks them in this book and renders them susceptible to a new solution.

The basic thesis of *The Elementary Forms*, considered apart from its stature as a contribution to the sociology of knowledge, is that the origin of religion is neither in animism nor in naturism but in society. Durkheim follows his usual careful procedure, first defining his terms in a way that makes unmistakable what he means, for example, by his prime concept, the concept of religion. Religion does not necessarily carry with it a connotation of the supernatural. Indeed, the idea of the supernatural is a relatively late development in the history of religion, and requires a notion of the natural in contrast to which it can be juxtaposed. Nor is the notion of divinity a necessary component of religion. There are religions like Buddhism in which the idea of spirits or gods is wholly absent and other religions in which it plays only a minor role. A definition of religion requires neither a supernature nor a deity but rather a recognition of the distinction, among the most definite and most striking of all distinctions, between the sacred and the profane.

The division of the world into two domains, the one containing all that is sacred, the other all that is profane, is the distinctive trait of religious thought; the beliefs, myths, dogmas and legends are either representations or systems of representations which express the nature of sacred things, the virtue and powers which are attributed to them, or their relations with each other and with profane things.*

There are things, in short, that are superior in dignity and power to the things that surround us in ordinary life, and these things comprise the elements of religion.

There is no mistaking the sacred. All societies have sacred objects and all the individuals who belong to these societies know without hesitation what these objects are and how they are to be treated. Only one additional observation need be made and that concerns the distinction between religion and magic. For magic, too, the distinction between the sacred and the profane obtains. The two phenomena would seem to be similar and this in spite of the repugnance that exists between religion and magic. The difference is that, wherever there is religion, there is an organized group of people united by their common perceptions of the sacred and carrying on the activities appropriate to these perceptions. Wherever there is religion, in short, there is also a church, whereas no similar group appears in the case of magic. The definition of religion that Durkheim will use, therefore, is the following: "A religion is a unified system of beliefs and practices relative to sacred things, that is to say, things set apart and forbidden—beliefs and practices which unite into one single moral community called a Church, all those who adhere to them."† Already we see, as Durkheim says, that religion is "an eminently collective thing."

The definition having been established, Durkheim turns next to a task of refutation. He has to refute the

*Ibid., p. 52.
†Ibid., p. 62.

extant theories of the origin of religion, particularly the theory of animism, espoused by Tylor and Spencer, and naturism, supported by Max Müller and others. This Durkheim does without difficulty and with many insights along the way, including several on the ability of language to create things, so to speak, that are not there. ("Language thus superimposes upon the material world, such as it is revealed to our senses, a new world, composed wholly of spiritual beings which it has created out of nothing and which have been considered as the causes determining physical phenomena ever since.") *

The key to the understanding of the origin of religion is the totem and the totemic principle. The totem is the symbol of the name and identity of a clan or tribe, and therefore of a society. It is society that creates the totem and the totem, in turn, serves *par excellence* as the basis of the sacred. Making many references to the publications of the American Bureau of Ethnology, and most especially to the work of the American anthropologist Lewis Henry Morgan, Durkheim undertakes an extensive analysis of totemism in the most primitive societies both in America and in Australia. He gives his highest praise, perhaps, to Spencer and Gillen, for their thoroughgoing studies, *The Native Tribes of Central Australia* and *The Northern Tribes of Central Australia,* and to the German missionary Carl Strehlow, who also studied these central Australian societies, and did so in great depth. It is Australia that becomes the theatre of Durkheim's own attention because the societies there exhibit a homogeneity without which comparison would be difficult and even fallacious, because the documents are more complete, and because one finds there—especially among the Arunta—religion in its simplest and most primitive form.

It is not necessary to follow Durkheim through his

*Ibid., p. 96.

detailed analysis of totemism in Australia. It goes on for many pages, some of which, it must be admitted, are tedious in their dedication to the details of belief and idea, of rite and ceremony. Durkheim, though not himself a "field" man in anthropology, in the sense that he never carried on anthropological research himself, nevertheless plunders the literature available to him for facts from which he will arrive at his sociological conclusions. His pages are rich in footnotes and his study is a memorial of the ability of a gifted man to utilize the work of others in the pursuit of his own designs. This remark intends no animadversion either on the researcher who collects the facts or the synthesizer who utilizes them. It does intend an observation on the importance of the distinction. The patient historian who studies the documents of a particular historical event, or even discovers them in some damp basement, contributes no less—and no more—to the progress of knowledge than the brilliant theoretician who, unacquainted with the basement, seizes upon the detail discovered there, and puts together, along with facts from other basements and attics of society, a philosophy of history, or, as in Durkheim's case, a sociology of religion. Given the importance of religion in human life, the distance between a philosophy of history and a sociology of religion is not very great.

The importance of the totem can hardly be overemphasized. It is at once emblem and heraldic device; it is reproduced on canoes, utensils, and tombs; it is imprinted on the flesh of the Australian primitive. But the totem is not merely name and emblem, not merely a collective label. It is also that to which the sacred is attached, that which helps to distinguish the sacred from the profane, and that, in consequence, which plays a central role in the origin of primitive religion. But the totem stems from society; it is a symbol of the group, and it reflects that group in the religion it creates. Religion, in short, is a social phenomenon. About the totem myths and ceremonies arise, and so we see it affecting both belief and rite, the two different but equally basic components of religion. Before the birth of the gods, the totem performs the service that will later become the responsibility of these divinities. The gods themselves are products of society and society has an "aptitude" for creating them.

This theory of the origin of religion escapes the difficulties of alternative theories. As Durkheim says:

> Religion ceases to be an inexplicable hallucination and takes a foothold in reality. In fact, we can say that the believer is not deceived when he believes in the existence of a moral power upon which he depends and from which he receives all that is best in himself: this power exists, it is society.*

Even the idea of the soul is socially derived; it is *mana* individualized; it is the internal expression or representation of the collective soul of the group. If the soul is immortal, the immortality too can be explained only by an appeal to society. For men observe that, whereas the individual is mortal, the life of society is a continuous process. The man dies, but his clan survives, and it is this survival that he translates back into his own consciousness and believes that his own soul, partaking of the survival power of the group, is also immortal. One believes in the immortality of the soul because it makes intelligible the continuity of the collective life.

Throughout his discussion, though never in a wholly systematic or complete way, Durkheim returns to his view of the social origins of the categories of thought. The concept of kind, for example, or class, has a clearly social origin. We distinguish ourselves from others, members of our tribes or clans from members of differ-

Ibid., p. 257.

ent ones, one society from another. "In all probability, we would never have thought of uniting the beings of the universe into homogeneous groups, called classes, if we had not had the example of human societies before our eyes."* Similarly for the ideas of cause, force, and power. The notion of power, for example, could hardly appear without such ideas as ascendancy, mastership, domination, dependence, and subordination. All of these ideas are social. And even further:

> It is society which classifies beings into superiors and inferiors, into commanding masters and obeying servants; it is society which confers upon the former the singular property which makes the command efficacious and which makes *power*. So everything tends to prove that the first powers of which the human mind had any idea were those which societies have established in organizing themselves; it is in their image that the powers of the physical world have been conceived.†

The categories in which our knowledge of the external world is packaged, in short, depends upon a prior knowledge of society, a prior knowledge of social forms and phenomena.

But it is not only the categories that are of social origin. Science itself has this source, through religion, of which it is only a superior manifestation:

> We have even seen that the essential ideas of scientific logic are of religious origin. It is true that in order to utilize them, science gives them a new elaboration; it purges them of all accidental elements; in a general way, it brings a spirit of criticism into all its doings, which religion ignores; it surrounds itself

Ibid., p. 173.
†*Ibid.*, p. 409.

with precautions to "escape precipitation and bias," and to hold aside the passions, prejudices and all subjective influences. But these perfectionings of method are not enough to differentiate it from religion. In this regard, both pursue the same end; scientific thought is only a more perfect form of religious thought. Thus it seems natural that the second should progressively retire before the first, as this becomes better fitted to perform the task.*

Durkheim recognizes, of course, that this conclusion is repugnant to many minds, but for him it is a simple result of his analysis and explains, in fact, the tension that exists between science and religion. Although religion will continue to exist, it must always retreat as science explains more and more of the natural world.

We can do no better, in ending this brief and unavoidably superficial account of Durkheim's book on the origin of religion, than to quote a paragraph from his Conclusion that summarizes his theory and the concluding sentence of which is as stark and as forceful as anything to have come from his pen:

As we have progressed, we have established the fact that the fundamental categories of thought, and consequently of science, are of religious origin. We have seen that the same is true for magic and consequently for the different processes which have issued from it. On the other hand, it has long been known that, up until a relatively advanced moment of evolution, moral and legal rules have been indistinguishable from ritual prescriptions. In summing up, then, it may be said that nearly all the great social institutions have been born in religion. Now in order that these principal aspects of the collective life may have commenced by being only varied aspects of the religious life, it is obviously necessary that the religious

*Ibid., p. 477.

life be the eminent form and, as it were, the concentrated expression of the whole collective life. If religion has given birth to all that is essential in society, it is because the idea of society is the soul of religion.*

"The idea of society is the soul of religion." This, in a single sentence, expresses the principal thesis of Durkheim's book. In his brilliant Conclusion, which we now reprint in its entirety, he once more draws out the implications of this thesis, discusses the intricate relationship between science and religion, shows that science itself has a religious origin, and finally stresses again the social character of the concepts and categories of the human understanding. To read it is to participate in some of the greatest moments in the history of social thought.

Conclusion†

At the beginning of this work we announced that the religion whose study we were taking up contained within it the most characteristic elements of the religious life. The exactness of this proposition may now be verified. Howsoever simple the system which we have studied may be, we have found within it all the great ideas and the principal ritual attitudes which are at the basis of even the most advanced religions: the division of things into sacred and profane, the notions of the soul, of spirits, of mythical personalities, and of a national and even international divinity, a negative cult with ascetic practices which are its exaggerated form, rites of oblation and communion, imitative rites, com-

*Ibid., p. 466.
†Ibid., pp. 462–96.

memorative rites and expiatory rites; nothing essential is lacking. We are thus in a position to hope that the results at which we have arrived are not peculiar to totemism alone, but can aid us in an understanding of what religion in general is.

It may be objected that one single religion, whatever its field of extension may be, is too narrow a base for such an induction. We have not dreamed for a moment of ignoring the fact that an extended verification may add to the authority of a theory, but it is equally true that when a law has been proven by one well-made experiment, this proof is valid universally. If in one single case a scientist succeeded in finding out the secret of the life of even the most protoplasmic creature that can be imagined, the truths thus obtained would be applicable to all living beings, even the most advanced. Then if, in our studies of these very humble societies, we have really succeeded in discovering some of the elements out of which the most fundamental religious notions are made up, there is no reason for not extending the most general results of our researches to other religions. In fact, it is inconceivable that the same effect may be due now to one cause, now to another, according to the circumstances, unless the two causes are at bottom only one. A single idea cannot express one reality here and another one there, unless the duality is only apparent. If among certain peoples the ideas of sacredness, the soul and God are to be explained sociologically, it should be presumed scientifically that, in principle, the same explanation is valid for all the peoples among whom these same ideas are found with the same essential characteristics. Therefore, supposing that we have not been deceived, certain at least of our conclusions can be legitimately generalized. The moment has come to disengage these. And an induction of this sort, having at its foundation a clearly defined experiment, is less adventurous than many summary generalizations which, while attempting to reach the essence of religion at once, without resting upon the careful analysis of any religion in particular, greatly risk losing themselves in space.

I   The theorists who have undertaken to explain religion in rational terms have generally seen in it before all else a system of ideas, corresponding to some determined object. This object has been conceived in a multitude of ways: nature, the infinite, the unknowable, the ideal, etc.; but these differences matter but little. In any case, it was the conceptions and beliefs which were considered as the essential elements of religion. As for the rites, from this point of view they appear to be only an external translation, contingent and material, of these internal states which alone pass as having any intrinsic value. This conception is so commonly held that generally the disputes of which religion is the theme turn about the question whether it can conciliate itself with science or not, that is to say, whether or not there is a place beside our scientific knowledge for another form of thought which would be specifically religious.

But the believers, the men who lead the religious life and have a direct sensation of what it really is, object to this way of regarding it, saying that it does not correspond to their daily experience. In fact, they feel that the real function of religion is not to make us think, to enrich our knowledge, nor to add to the conceptions which we owe to science others of another origin and another character, but rather, it is to make us act, to aid us to live. The believer who has communicated with his god is not merely a man who sees new truths of which the unbeliever is ignorant; he is a man who is stronger. He feels within him more force, either to endure the trials of existence, or to conquer them. It is as though he were raised above the miseries of the world, because he is raised above his condition as a mere man; he believes that he is saved from evil, under whatever form he may conceive his evil. The first article in every creed is the belief in salvation by faith. But it is hard to see how a mere idea could have this efficacy. An idea is in reality only a part of ourselves; then how could it confer upon us powers superior to those which we have of our own nature? Howsoever rich it might be in affective virtues, it could add nothing to our natural vitality; for it could only release the motive powers which are within us, neither creating them nor increasing them. From the mere fact that we consider an object worthy of being loved and sought after, it does not follow that we feel ourselves stronger afterwards; it is also necessary that this object set free energies superior to these which we ordinarily have at our command and also that we have some means of making these enter into us and unite themselves to our interior lives. Now for that, it is not enough that we think of them; it is also indispensable that we place ourselves within their sphere of action, and that we set ourselves where we may best feel their influence; in a word, it is necessary that we act, and that we repeat the acts thus necessary every time we feel the need of renewing their effects. From this point of view, it is readily seen how that group of regularly repeated acts which form the cult get their importance. In fact, whoever has really practised a religion knows very well that it is the cult which gives rise to these impressions of joy, of interior peace, of serenity, of enthusiasm which are, for the believer, an experimental proof of his beliefs. The cult is not simply a system of signs by which the faith is outwardly translated; it is a collection of the means by which this is created and recreated periodically. Whether it consists in material acts or mental operations, it is always this which is efficacious.

Our entire study rests upon this postulate that the unanimous sentiment of the believers of all times cannot be purely illusory. Together with a recent apologist of the faith we admit that these religious beliefs rest upon a specific experience whose demonstrative value is, in one sense, not one bit inferior to that of scientific experiments, though different from them. We, too, think that "a tree is known by its fruits," and that fertility is the best proof of what the roots are worth. But from the fact that a "religious experience," if we choose to call it this, does exist and that it has a certain foundation—and, by the way, is there any experience which has none?—it does not follow that the reality which is its foundation conforms objectively to the idea which believers have of it. The very fact that the fashion in which it has been conceived has varied infinitely in different times is enough to prove that none of these conceptions express it adequately. If a scientist states it as an axiom that the sensations of heat and light which we feel correspond to some objective cause, he does not conclude that this is what it appears to the senses to be. Likewise, even if the impressions which the faithful feel are not imaginary, still they are in no way privileged intuitions; there is no reason for believing that they inform us better upon the nature of their object than do ordinary sensations upon the nature of bodies and their properties. In order to discover what this object consists of, we must submit them to an examination and elaboration analogous to that which has substituted for the sensuous idea of the world another which is scientific and conceptual.

This is precisely what we have tried to do, and we have seen that this reality, which mythologies have represented under so many different forms, but which is the universal and eternal objective cause of the sensations *sui generis* out of which religious experience is made, is society. We have shown what moral forces it develops and how it awakens this sentiment of a refuge, of a shield and of a guardian support which attaches the believer to his cult. It is that which raises him outside himself; it is even that which made him. For that which makes a man is the totality of the intellectual property which constitutes civilization, and civilization is the work of society. Thus is explained the preponderating role of the cult in all religions, whichever they may be. This is because society cannot make its influence felt unless it is in action, and it is not in action unless the individuals who compose it are assembled together and act in common. It is by common action that it takes consciousness of itself and realizes its position; it is before all else an active co-operation. The collective ideas and sentiments are even possible only owing to these exterior movements which symbolize them, as we have established. Then it is action which dominates the religious life, because of the mere fact that it is society which is its source.

In addition to all the reasons which have been given to justify this conception, a final one may be added here, which is the result of our whole work. As we have progressed, we have established the fact that the fundamental categories of thought, and consequently of science, are of religious origin. We have seen that the same is true for magic and consequently for the different processes which have issued from it. On the other hand, it has long been known that up until a relatively advanced moment of evolution, moral and legal rules have been indistinguishable from ritual prescriptions. In summing up, then, it may be said that nearly all the great social institutions have been born in religion. Now in order that these principal aspects of the collective life may have commenced by being only varied aspects of the religious life, it is obviously necessary that the religious life be the eminent form and, as it were, the concentrated expression of the whole collective life. If religion has given birth to all that is essential in society, it is because the idea of society is the soul of religion.

Religious forces are therefore human forces, moral forces. It is true that since collective sentiments can become conscious of themselves only by fixing themselves upon external objects, they have not been able to take form without adopting some of their characteristics from other things: they have thus acquired a sort of physical nature; in this way they have come to mix themselves with the life of the material world, and then have considered themselves capable of explaining what passes there. But when they are considered only from this point of view and in this role, only their most superficial aspect is seen. In reality, the essential elements of which these collective sentiments are made have been borrowed by the understanding. It ordinarily seems that they should have a human character only when they are conceived under human forms; but even the most impersonal and the most anonymous are nothing else than objectified sentiments.

It is only by regarding religion from this angle that it is possible to see its real significance. If we stick closely to appearances, rites often give the effect of purely manual operations: they are anointings, washings, meals. To consecrate something, it is put in contact with a source of heat or electricity to warm or electrize it; the two processes employed are not essentially different. Thus understood, religious technique seems to be a sort of mystic mechanics. But these material manœuvres are only the external envelope under which the mental operations are hidden. Finally, there is no question of exercising a physical constraint upon blind and, incidentally, imaginary forces, but rather of reaching individual consciousnesses, of giving them a direction and of disciplining them. It is sometimes said that inferior religions are materialistic. Such an expression is inexact. All religions, even the crudest, are in a sense spiritualistic: for the powers they put in play are before all spiritual, and also their principal object is to act upon the moral life. Thus it is seen that whatever has been done in the name of religion cannot have been done in vain: for it is necessarily the society that did it, and it is humanity that has reaped the fruits.

But, it is said, what society is it that has thus made the basis of religion? Is it the real society, such as it is and acts before our very eyes, and with the legal and moral organization which it has laboriously fashioned during the course of history? This is full of defects and imperfections. In it, evil goes beside the good, injustice often reigns supreme, and the truth is often obscured by error. How could anything so crudely organized inspire the sentiments of love, the ardent enthusiasm and the spirit of abnegation which all religions claim of their followers? These perfect beings which are gods could not have taken their traits from so mediocre, and sometimes even so base a reality.

But, on the other hand, does someone think of a perfect society, where justice and truth would be sovereign, and from which evil in all its forms would be banished for ever? No one would deny that this is in close relations with the religious sentiment; for, they would say, it is towards the realization of this that all religions strive. But that society is not an empirical fact, definite and observable; it is a fancy, a dream with which men have lightened their sufferings, but in which they have never really lived. It is merely an idea which comes to express our more or less obscure aspirations towards the good, the beautiful and the ideal. Now these aspirations have their roots in us; they come from the very depths of our being; then there is nothing outside of us which can account for them. Moreover, they are already religious in themselves; thus it would seem that the ideal society presupposes religion, far from being able to explain it.

But, in the first place, things are arbitrarily simplified when religion is seen only on its idealistic side: in its way, it is realistic. There is no physical or moral ugliness, there are no vices or evils which do not have a special divinity. There are gods of theft and trickery, of lust and war, of sickness and of death. Christianity itself, howsoever high the idea which it has made of the divinity may be, has been obliged to give the spirit of evil a place in its mythology. Satan is an essential piece of the Christian system; even if he is an impure being, he is not a profane one. The anti-god is a god, inferior and subordinated, it is true, but nevertheless endowed with extended powers; he is even the object of rites, at least of negative ones. Thus religion, far from ignoring the real society and making abstraction of it, is in its image; it reflects all its aspects, even the most vulgar and the most repulsive. All is to be found there, and if in the majority of cases we see the good victorious over evil, life over death, the powers of light over the powers of darkness, it is because reality is not otherwise. If the relation between these two contrary forces were reversed, life would be impossible; but, as a matter of fact, it maintains itself and even tends to develop.

But if, in the midst of these mythologies and theologies we see reality clearly appearing, it is none the less true that it is found there only in an enlarged, transformed and idealized form. In this respect, the most primitive religions do not differ from the most recent and the most refined. For example, we have seen how the Arunta place at the beginning of time a mythical society whose organization exactly reproduces that which still exists to-day; it includes the same clans and phratries, it is under the same matrimonial rules and it practises the same rites. But the personages who compose it are ideal beings, gifted with powers and virtues to which common mortals cannot pretend. Their nature is not only higher, but it is different, since it is at once animal and human. The evil powers there undergo a similar metamorphosis: evil itself is, as it were, made sublime and idealized. The question now raises itself of whence this idealization comes.

Some reply that men have a natural faculty for idealizing, that is to say, of substituting for the real world another different one, to which they transport themselves by thought. But that is merely changing the terms of the problem; it is not resolving it or even advancing it. This systematic idealization is an essential characteristic of religions. Explaining them by an innate power of idealization is simply replacing one word by another which is the equivalent of the first; it is as if they said that men have made religions because they have a religious nature. Animals know only one world, the one which they perceive by experience, internal as well as external. Men alone have the faculty of conceiving the ideal, of adding something to the real. Now where does this singular privilege come from? Before making it an initial fact or a mysterious virtue which escapes science, we must be sure that it does not depend upon empirically determinable conditions.

The explanation of religion which we have proposed has precisely this advantage, that it gives an answer to this question. For our definition of the sacred is that it is something added to and above the real: now the ideal answers to this same definition; we cannot explain one without explaining the other. In fact, we have seen that if collective life awakens religious thought on reaching a certain degree of intensity, it is because it brings about a state of effervescence which changes the conditions of psychic activity. Vital energies are over-excited, passions more active, sensations stronger; there are even some which are produced only at this moment. A man does not recognize himself; he feels himself transformed and consequently he transforms the environment which surrounds him. In order to account for the very particular impressions which he receives, he attributes to the things with which he is in most direct contact properties which they have not, exceptional powers and virtues which the objects of every-day experience do not possess. In a word, above the real world where his profane life passes he has placed another which, in one sense, does not exist except in thought, but to which he attributes a higher sort of dignity than to the first. Thus, from a double point of view it is an ideal world.

The formation of the ideal world is therefore not an irreducible fact which escapes science; it depends upon conditions which observation can touch; it is a natural product of social life. For a society to become conscious of itself and maintain at the necessary degree of intensity the sentiments which it thus attains, it must assemble and concentrate itself. Now this concentration brings about an exaltation of the mental life which takes form in a group of ideal conceptions where is portrayed the new life thus awakened; they correspond to this new set of psychical forces which is added to those which we have at our disposition for the daily tasks of existence. A society can neither create itself nor recreate itself without at the same time creating an ideal. This creation is not a sort of work of supererogation for it, by which it would complete itself, being already formed; it is the act by which it is periodically made and remade. Therefore when some oppose the ideal society to the real society, like two antagonists which would lead us in opposite directions, they materialize and oppose abstractions. The ideal society is not outside of the real society; it is a part of it. Far from being divided between them as between two poles which mutually repel each other, we cannot hold to one without holding to the other. For a society is not made up merely of the mass of individuals who compose it, the ground which they occupy, the things which they use and the movements which they perform, but above all is the idea which it forms of itself. It is undoubtedly true that it hesitates over the manner in which it ought to conceive itself; it feels itself drawn in divergent directions. But these conflicts which break forth are not between the ideal and reality, but between two different ideals, that of yesterday and that of to-day, that which has the authority of tradition and that which has the hope of the future. There is surely a place for investigating whence these ideals evolve; but whatever solution may be given to this problem, it still remains that all passes in the world of the ideal.

Thus the collective ideal which religion expresses is far from being due to a vague innate power of the individual, but it is rather at the school of collective life that the individual has learned to idealize. It is in assimilating the ideals elaborated by society that he has become capable of conceiving the ideal. It is society which, by leading him within its sphere of action, has made him acquire the need of raising himself above the world of experience and has at the same time furnished him with the means of conceiving another. For society has constructed this new world in constructing itself, since it is society which this expresses. Thus both with the individual and in the group, the faculty of idealizing has nothing mysterious about it. It is not a sort of luxury which a man could get along without, but a condition of his very existence. He could not be a social being, that is to say, he could not be a man, if he had not acquired it. It is true that in incarnating themselves in individuals, collective ideals tend to individualize themselves. Each understands them after his own fashion and marks them with his own stamp; he suppresses certain elements and adds others. Thus the personal ideal disengages itself from the social ideal in proportion as the individual personality develops itself and becomes an autonomous source of action. But if we wish to understand this aptitude, so singular in appearance, of living outside of reality, it is enough to connect it with the social conditions upon which it depends.

Therefore it is necessary to avoid seeing in this theory of religion a simple restatement of historical materialism: that would be misunderstanding our thought to an extreme degree. In showing that religion is something essentially social, we do not mean to say that it confines itself to translating into another language the material forms of society and its immediate vital necessities. It is true that we take it as evident that social life depends upon its material foundation and bears its mark, just as the mental life of an individual depends upon his nervous system and in fact his whole organism. But collective consciousness is something more than a mere epiphenomenon of its morphological basis, just as individual consciousness is something more than a simple efflorescence of the nervous system. In order that the former may appear, a synthesis *sui generis* of particular consciousnesses is required. Now this synthesis has the effect of disengaging a whole world of sentiments, ideas and images which, once born, obey laws all their own. They attract each other, repel each other, unite, divide themselves, and multiply, though these combinations are not commanded and necessitated by the condition of the underlying reality. The life thus brought into being even enjoys so great an independence that it sometimes indulges in manifestations with no purpose or utility of any sort, for the mere pleasure of affirming itself. We have shown that this is often precisely the case with ritual activity and mythological thought.

But if religion is the product of social causes, how can we explain the individual cult and the universalistic character of certain religions? If it is born *in foro externo,* how has it been able to pass into the inner conscience of the individual and penetrate there ever more and more profoundly? If it is the work of definite and individualized societies, how has it been able to detach itself from them, even to the point of being conceived as something common to all humanity?

In the course of our studies, we have met with the germs of individual religion and of religious cosmopolitanism, and we have seen how they were formed; thus we possess the more general elements of the reply which is to be given to this double question.

We have shown how the religious force which animates the clan particularizes itself, by incarnating itself in particular consciousnesses. Thus secondary sacred beings are formed; each individual has his own, made in his own image, associated to his own intimate life, bound up with his own destiny; it is the soul, the individual totem, the protecting ancestor, etc. These beings are the object of rites which the individual can celebrate by himself, outside of any group; this is the first form of the individual cult. To be sure, it is only a very rudimentary cult; but since the personality of the individual is still only slightly marked, and but little value is attributed to it, the cult which expresses it could hardly be expected to be very highly developed as yet. But as individuals have differentiated themselves more and more and the value of an individual has increased, the corresponding cult has taken a relatively greater place in the totality of the religious life and at the same time it is more fully closed to outside influences.

Thus the existence of individual cults implies nothing which contradicts or embarrasses the sociological interpretation of religion; for the religious forces to which it addresses itself are only the individualized forms of collective forces. Therefore, even when religion seems to be entirely within the individual conscience, it is still in society that it finds the living source from which it is nourished. We are now able to appreciate the value of the radical individualism which would make religion something purely individual: it misunderstands the fundamental conditions of the religious life. If up to the present it has remained in the stage of theoretical aspirations which have never been realized, it is because it is unrealizable. A philosophy may well be elaborated in the silence of the interior imagination, but not so a faith. For before all else, a faith is warmth, life, enthusiasm, the exaltation of the whole mental life, the raising of the individual above himself. Now how could he add to the energies which he possesses without going outside himself? How could he surpass himself merely by his own forces? The only source of life at which we can morally reanimate ourselves is that formed by the society of our fellow beings; the only moral forces with which we can sustain and increase our own are those which we get from others. Let us even admit that there really are beings more or less analogous to those which the mythologies represent. In order that they may exercise over souls the useful direction which is their reason for existence, it is necessary that men believe in them. Now these beliefs are active only when they are partaken by many. A man cannot retain them any length of time by a purely personal effort; it is not thus that they are born or that they are acquired; it is even doubtful if they can be kept under these conditions. In fact, a man who has a veritable faith feels an invincible need of spreading it: therefore he leaves his isolation, approaches others and seeks to convince them, and it is the ardour of the convictions which he arouses that strengthens his own. It would quickly weaken if it remained alone.

It is the same with religious universalism as with this individualism. Far from being an exclusive attribute of certain very great religions, we have found it, not at the base, it is true, but at the summit of the Australian system. Bunjil, Daramulum or Baiame are not simple tribal gods; each of them is recognized by a number of different tribes. In a sense, their cult is international. This conception is therefore very near to that found in the most recent theologies. So certain writers have felt it their duty to deny its authenticity, howsoever incontestable this may be.

And we have been able to show how this has been formed.

Neighboring tribes of a similar civilization cannot fail to be in constant relations with each other. All sorts of circumstances give an occasion for it: besides commerce, which is still rudimentary, there are marriages; these international marriages are very common in Australia. In the course of these meetings, men naturally become conscious of the moral relationship which united them. They have the same social organization, the same division into phratries, clans and matrimonial classes; they practise the same rites of initiation, or wholly similar ones. Mutual loans and treaties result in reinforcing these spontaneous resemblances. The gods to which these manifestly identical institutions were attached could hardly have remained distinct in their minds. Everything tended to bring them together and consequently, even supposing that each tribe elaborated the notion independently, they must necessarily have tended to confound themselves with each other. Also, it is probable that it was in inter-tribal assemblies that they were first conceived. For they are chiefly the gods of initiation, and in the initiation ceremonies, the different tribes are usually represented. So if sacred beings are formed which are connected with no geographically determined society, that is not because they have an extra-social origin. It is because there are other groups above these geographically determined ones, whose contours are less clearly marked: they have no fixed frontiers, but include all sorts of more or less neighbouring and related tribes. The particular social life thus created tends to spread itself over an area with no definite limits. Naturally the mythological personages who correspond to it have the same character; their sphere of influence is not limited; they go beyond the particular tribes and their territory. They are the great international gods.

Now there is nothing in this situation which is peculiar to Australian societies. There is no people and no state which is not a part of another society, more or less unlimited, which embraces all the peoples and all the States with which the first comes in contact, either directly or indirectly; there is no national life which is not dominated by a collective life of an international nature. In proportion as we advance in history, these international groups acquire a greater importance and extent. Thus we see how, in certain cases, this universalistic tendency has been able to develop itself to the point of affecting not only the higher ideas of the religious system, but even the principles upon which it rests.

II   Thus there is something eternal in religion which is destined to survive all the particular symbols in which religious thought has successively enveloped itself. There can be no society which does not feel the need of upholding and reaffirming at regular intervals the collective sentiments and the collective ideas which make its unity and its personality. Now this moral remaking cannot be achieved except by the means of reunions, assemblies and meetings where the individuals, being closely united to one another, reaffirm in common their common sentiments; hence come ceremonies which do not differ from regular religious ceremonies either in their object, the results which they produce, or the processes employed to attain these results. What essential difference is there between an assembly of Christians celebrating the principal dates of the life of Christ, or of Jews remembering the exodus from Egypt or the promulgation of the decalogue, and a reunion of citizens commemorating the promulgation of a new moral or legal system or some great event in the national life?

If we find a little difficulty to-day in imagining what these feasts and ceremonies of the future could consist in, it is because we are going through a stage of transition and moral mediocrity. The great things of the past which filled our fathers with enthusiasm do not excite the same ardour in us, either because they have come into common usage to such an extent that we are unconscious of them, or else because they no longer answer to our actual aspirations; but as yet there is nothing to replace them. We can no longer impassionate ourselves for the principles in the name of which Christianity recommended to masters that they treat their slaves humanely, and, on the other hand, the idea which it has formed of human equality and fraternity seems to us to-day to leave too large a place of unjust inequalities. Its pity for the outcast seems to us too Platonic; we desire another which would be more practicable; but as yet we cannot clearly see what it should be nor how it could be realized in facts. In a word, the old gods are growing old or already dead, and others are not yet born. This is what rendered vain the attempt of Comte with the old historic souvenirs artificially revived: it is life itself, and not a dead past which can produce a living cult. But this state of incertitude and confused agitation cannot last for ever. A day will come when our societies will know again those hours of creative effervescence, in the course of which new ideas arise and new formulae are found which serve for a while as a guide to humanity; and when these hours shall have been passed through once, men will spontaneously feel the need of reliving them from time to time in thought, that is to say, of keeping alive their memory by means of celebrations which regularly reproduce their fruits. We have already seen how the French Revolution established a whole cycle of holidays to keep the principles with which it was inspired in a state of perpetual youth. If this institution quickly fell away, it was because the revolutionary faith lasted but a moment, and deceptions and discouragements rapidly succeeded the first moments of enthusiasm. But though the work may have miscarried, it enables us to imagine what might have happened in other conditions; and everything leads us to believe that it will be taken up again sooner or later. There are no gospels which are immortal, but neither is there any reason for believing that humanity is incapable of inventing new ones. As to the question of what symbols this new faith will express itself with, whether they will resemble those of the past or not, and whether or not they will be more adequate for the reality which they seek to translate, that is something which surpasses the human faculty of foresight and which does not appertain to the principal question.

But feasts and rites, in a word, the cult, are not the whole religion. This is not merely a system of practices, but also a system of ideas whose object is to explain the world; we have seen that even the humblest have their cosmology. Whatever connection there may be between these two elements of the religious life, they are still quite different. The one is turned towards action, which it demands and regulates; the other is turned towards thought, which it enriches and organizes. Then they do not depend upon the same conditions, and consequently it may be asked if the second answers to necessities as universal and as permanent as the first.

When specific characteristics are attributed to religious thought, and when it is believed that its function is to express, by means peculiar to itself, an aspect of reality which evades ordinary knowledge as well as science, one naturally refuses to admit that religion can ever abandon its speculative role. But our analysis of the facts does not seem to have shown this specific quality of religion. The religion which we have just studied is one of those whose symbols are the most disconcerting for the reason. There all appears mysterious. These beings which belong to the most heterogeneous groups at the same time, who multiply without ceasing to be one, who divide without diminishing, all seem, at first view, to belong to an entirely different world from the one where we live; some have even gone so far as to say that the mind which constructed them ignored the laws of logic completely. Perhaps the contrast between reason and faith has never been more thorough. Then if there has ever been a moment in history when their heterogeneousness should have stood out clearly, it is here. But contrary to all appearances, as we have pointed out, the realities to which religious speculation is then applied are the same as those which later serve as the subject of reflection for philosophers: they are nature, man, society. The mystery which appears to surround them is wholly superficial and disappears before a more painstaking observation: it is enough merely to set aside the veil with which mythological imagination has covered them for them to appear such as they really are. Religion sets itself to translate these realities into an intelligible language which does not differ in nature from that employed by science; the attempt is made by both to connect things with each other, to establish internal relations between them, to classify them and to systematize them. We have even seen that the essential ideas of scientific logic are of religious origin. It is true that in order to utilize them, science gives them a new elaboration; it purges them of all accidental elements; in a general way, it brings a spirit of criticism into all its doings, which religion ignores; it surrounds itself with precautions to "escape precipitation and bias," and to hold aside the passions, prejudices and all subjective influences. But these perfectionings of method are not enough to differentiate it from religion. In this regard, both pursue the same end; scientific thought is only a more perfect form of religious thought. Thus it seems natural that the second should progressively retire before the first, as this becomes better fitted to perform the task.

And there is no doubt that this regression has taken place in the course of history. Having left religion, science tends to substitute itself for this latter in all that which concerns the cognitive and intellectual functions. Christianity has already definitely consecrated this substitution in the order of material things. Seeing in matter that which is profane before all else, it readily left the knowledge of this to another discipline, *tradidit mundum hominum disputationi,* "He gave the world over to the disputes of men"; it is thus that the natural sciences have been able to establish themselves and make their authority recognized without very great difficulty. But it could not give up the world of souls so easily; for it is before all over souls that the god of the Christians aspires to reign. That is why the idea of submitting the psychic life to science produced the effect of a sort of profanation for a long time; even to-day it is repugnant to many minds. However, experimental and comparative psychology is founded and to-day we must reckon with it. But the world of the religious and moral life is still forbidden. The great majority of men continue to believe that here there is an order of things which the mind cannot penetrate except by very special ways. Hence comes the active resistance which is met with every time that someone tries to treat religious and moral phenomena scientifically. But in spite of these oppositions, these attempts are constantly repeated and this persistence even allows us to foresee that this final barrier will finally give way and that science will establish herself as mistress even in this reserved region.

That is what the conflict between science and religion really amounts to. It is said that science denies religion in principle. But religion exists; it is a system of given facts; in a word, it is a reality. How could science deny this reality? Also, in so far as religion is action, and in so far as it is a means of making men live, science could not take its place, for even if this expresses life, it does not create it; it may well seek to explain the faith, but by that very act it presupposes it. Thus there is no conflict except upon one limited point. Of the two functions which religion originally fulfilled, there is one, and only one, which tends to escape it more and more: that is its speculative function. That which science refuses to grant to religion is not its right to exist, but its right to dogmatize upon the nature of things and the special competence which it claims for itself for knowing man and the world. As a matter of fact, it does not know itself. It does not even know what it is made of, nor to what need it answers. It is itself a subject for science, so far is it from being able to make the law for science! And from another point of view, since there is no proper subject for religious speculation outside that reality to which scientific reflection is applied, it is evident that this former cannot play the same role in the future that it has played in the past.

However, it seems destined to transform itself rather than to disappear.

We have said that there is something eternal in religion: it is the cult and the faith. Men cannot celebrate ceremonies for which they see no reason, nor can they accept a faith which they in no way understand. To spread itself or merely to maintain itself, it must be justified, that is to say, a theory must be made of it. A theory of this sort must undoubtedly be founded upon the different sciences, from the moment when these exist; first of all, upon the social sciences, for religious faith has its origin in society; then upon psychology, for society is a synthesis of human consciousnesses; and finally upon the sciences of nature, for man and society are a part of the universe and can be abstracted from it only artificially. But howsoever important these facts taken from the constituted sciences may be, they are not enough; for faith is before all else an impetus to action, while science, no matter how far it may be pushed, always remains at a distance from this. Science is fragmentary and incomplete; it advances but slowly and is never finished; but life cannot wait. The theories which are destined to make men live and act are therefore obliged to pass science and complete it prematurely. They are possible only when the practical exigencies and the vital necessities which we feel without distinctly conceiving them push thought in advance, beyond that which science permits us to affirm. Thus religions, even the most rational and laicized, cannot and never will be able to dispense with a particular form of speculation which, though having the same subjects as science itself, cannot be really scientific: the obscure intuitions of sensations and sentiment too often take the place of logical reasons. On one side, this speculation resembles that which we meet with in the religions of the past; but on another, it is different. While claiming and exercising the right of going beyond science, it must commence by knowing this and by inspiring itself with it. Ever since the authority of science was established, it must be reckoned with; one can go farther than it under the pressure of necessity, but he must take his direction from it. He can affirm nothing that it denies, deny nothing that it affirms, and establish nothing that is not directly or indirectly founded upon principles taken from it. From now on, the faith no longer exercises the same hegemony as formerly over the system of ideas that we may continue to call religion. A rival power rises up before it which, being born of it, ever after submits it to its criticism and control. And everything makes us foresee that this control will constantly become more extended and efficient, while no limit can be assigned to its future influence.

III   But if the fundamental notions of science are of a religious origin, how has religion been able to bring them forth? At first sight, one does not see what relations there can be between religion and logic. Or, since the reality which religious thought expresses is society, the question can be stated in the following terms, which make the entire difficulty appear even better: what has been able to make social life so important a source for the logical life? It seems as though nothing could have predestined it to this role, for it certainly was not to satisfy their speculative needs that men associated themselves together.

Perhaps we shall be found over-bold in attempting so complex a question here. To treat it as it should be treated, the sociological conditions of knowledge should be known much better than they actually are; we are only beginning to catch glimpses of some of them.

However, the question is so grave, and so directly implied in all that has preceded, that we must make an effort not to leave it without an answer. Perhaps it is not impossible, even at present, to state some general principles which may at least aid in the solution.

Logical thought is made up of concepts. Seeking how society can have played a role in the genesis of logical thought thus reduces itself to seeking how it can have taken a part in the formation of concepts.

If, as is ordinarily the case, we see in the concept only a general idea, the problem appears insoluble. By his own power, the individual can compare his conceptions and images, disengage that which they have in common, and thus, in a word, generalize. Then it is hard to see why this generalization should be possible only in and through society. But, in the first place, it is inadmissible that logical thought is characterized only by the greater extension of the conceptions of which it is made up. If particular ideas have nothing logical about them, why should it be different with general ones? The general exists only in the particular; it is the particular simplified and impoverished. Then the first could have no virtues or privileges which the second has not. Inversely, if conceptual thought can be applied to the class, species or variety, howsoever restricted these may be, why can it not be extended to the individual, that is to say, to the limit towards which the conception tends, proportionately as its extension diminishes? As a matter of fact, there are many concepts which have only individuals as their object. In every sort of religion, gods are individualities distinct from each other; however, they are conceived, not perceived. Each people represents its historic or legendary heroes in fashions which vary with the time. Finally, every one of us forms an idea of the individuals with whom he comes in contact, of their character, of their appearance, their distinctive traits and their moral and physical temperaments: these notions, too, are real concepts. It is true that in general they are formed crudely enough; but even among scientific concepts, are there a great many that are perfectly adequate for their object? In this direction, there are only differences of degree between them.

Therefore the concept must be defined by other characteristics. It is opposed to sensual representations of every order—sensations, perceptions or images—by the following properties.

Sensual representations are in a perpetual flux; they come after each other like the waves of a river, and even during the time that they last, they do not remain the same thing. Each of them is an integral part of the precise instant when it takes place. We are never sure of again finding a perception such as we experienced it the first time; for if the thing perceived has not changed, it is we who are no longer the same. On the contrary, the concept is, as it were, outside of time and change; it is in the depths below all this agitation; it might be said that it is in a different portion of the mind, which is serener and calmer. It does not move of itself, by an internal and spontaneous evolution, but, on the contrary, it resists change. It is a manner of thinking that, at every moment of time, is fixed and crystallized. In so far as it is what it ought to be, it is immutable. If it changes, it is not because it is its nature to do so, but because we have discovered some imperfection in it; it is because it had to be rectified. The system of concepts with which we think in every-day life is that expressed by the vocabulary of our mother tongue; for every word translates a concept. Now language is something fixed; it changes but very slowly, and consequently it is the same with the conceptual system which it expresses. The scholar finds himself in the same situation in regard to the special terminology employed by the science to which he has consecrated himself, and hence in regard to the special scheme of concepts to which this terminology corresponds. It is true that he can make innovations, but these are always a sort of violence done to the established ways of thinking.

And at the same time that it is relatively immutable, the concept is universal, or at least capable of becoming so. A concept is not my concept; I hold it in common with other men, or, in any case, can communicate it to them. It is impossible for me to make a sensation pass from my consciousness into that of another; it holds closely to my organism and personality and cannot be detached from them. All that I can do is to invite others to place themselves before the same object as myself and to leave themselves to its action. On the other hand, conversation and all intellectual communication between men is an exchange of concepts. The concept is an essentially impersonal representation; it is through it that human intelligences communicate.

The nature of the concept, thus defined, bespeaks its origin. If it is common to all, it is the work of the community. Since it bears the mark of no particular mind, it is clear that it was elaborated by a unique intelligence, where all others meet each other, and after a fashion, come to nourish themselves. If it has more stability than sensations or images, it is because the collective representations are more stable than the individual ones; for while an individual is conscious even of the slight changes which take place in his environment, only events of a greater gravity can succeed in affecting the mental status of a society. Every time that we are in the presence of a *type* of thought or action which is imposed uniformly upon particular wills or intelligences, this pressure exercised over the individual betrays the intervention of the group. Also, as we have already said, the concepts with which we ordinarily think are those of our vocabulary. Now it is unquestionable that language, and consequently the system of concepts which it translates, is the product of a collective elaboration. What it expresses is the manner in which society as a whole represents the facts of experience. The ideas which correspond to the diverse elements of language are thus collective representations.

Even their contents bear witness to the same fact. In fact, there are scarcely any words among those which we usually employ whose meaning does not pass, to a greater or less extent, the limits of our personal experience. Very frequently a term expresses things which we have never perceived or experiences which we have never had or of which we have never been the witnesses. Even when we know some of the objects which it concerns, it is only as particular examples that they serve to illustrate the idea which they would never have been able to form by themselves. Thus there is a great deal of knowledge condensed in the word which I never collected, and which is not individual; it even surpasses me to such an extent that I cannot even completely appropriate all its results. Which of us knows all the words of the language he speaks and the entire signification of each?

This remark enables us to determine the sense in which we mean to say that concepts are collective representations. If they belong to a whole social group, it is not because they represent the average of the corresponding individual representations; for in that case they would be poorer than the latter in intellectual content, while, as a matter of fact, they contain much that surpasses the knowledge of the average individual. They are not abstractions which have a reality only in particular consciousnesses, but they are as concrete representations as an individual could form of his own personal environment: they correspond to the way in which this very special being, society, considers the things of its own proper experience. If, as a matter of fact, the concepts are nearly always general ideas, and if they express categories and classes rather than particular objects, it is because the unique and variable characteristics of things interest society but rarely; because of its very extent, it can scarcely be affected by more than their general and permanent qualities. Therefore it is to this aspect of affairs that it gives its attention: it is a part of its nature to see things in large and under the aspect which they ordinarily have. But this generality is not necessary for them, and, in any case, even when these representations have the generic character which they ordinarily have, they are the work of society and are enriched by its experience.

That is what makes conceptual thought so valuable for us. If concepts were only general ideas, they would not enrich knowledge a great deal, for, as we have already pointed out, the general contains nothing more than the particular. But if before all else they are collective representations, they add to that which we can learn by our own personal experience all that wisdom and science which the group has accumulated in the course of centuries. Thinking by concepts is not merely seeing reality on its most general side, but it is projecting a light upon the sensation which illuminates it, penetrates it and transforms it. Conceiving something is both learning its essential elements better and also locating it in its place; for each civilization has its organized system of concepts which characterizes it. Before this scheme of ideas, the individual is in the same situation as the *vous (nous)* of Plato before the world of Ideas. He must assimilate them to himself, for he must have them to hold intercourse with others; but the assimilation is always imperfect. Each of us sees them after his own fashion. There are some which escape us completely and remain outside of our circle of vision; there are others of which we perceive certain aspects only. There are even a great many which we pervert in holding, for as they are collective by nature, they cannot become individualized without being retouched, modified, and consequently falsified. Hence comes the great trouble we have in understanding each other, and the fact that we even lie to each other without wishing to: it is because we all use the same words without giving them the same meaning.

We are now able to see what the part of society in the genesis of logical thought is. This is possible only from the moment when, above the fugitive conceptions which they owe to sensuous experience, men have succeeded in conceiving a whole world of stable ideas, the common ground of all intelligences. In fact, logical thinking is always impersonal thinking, and is also thought *sub specie æternitatis*—as thought for all time. Impersonality and stability are the two characteristics of truth. Now logical life evidently presupposes that men know, at least confusedly, that there is such a thing as truth, distinct from sensuous appearances. But how have they been able to arrive at this conception? We generally talk as though it should have spontaneously presented itself to them from the moment they opened their eyes upon the world. However, there is nothing in immediate experience which could suggest it; everything even contradicts it. Thus the child and the animal have no suspicion of it. History shows that it has taken centuries for it to disengage and establish itself. In our Western world, it was with the great thinkers of Greece that it first became clearly conscious of itself and of the consequences which it implies; when the discovery was made, it caused an amazement which Plato has translated into magnificent language. But if it is only at this epoch that the idea is expressed in philosophic formulae, it was necessarily pre-existent in the stage of an obscure sentiment. Philosophers have sought to elucidate this sentiment, but they have not succeeded. In order that they might reflect upon it and analyse it, it was necessary that it be given them, and that they seek to know whence it came, that is to say, in what experience it was founded. This is in collective experience. It is under the form of collective thought that impersonal thought is for the first time revealed to humanity; we cannot see by what other way this revelation could have been made. From the mere fact that society exists, there is also, outside of the individual sensations and images, a whole system of representations which enjoy marvellous properties. By means of them, men understand each other and intelligences grasp each other. They have within them a sort of force or moral ascendancy, in virtue of which they impose themselves upon individual minds. Hence the individual at least obscurely takes account of the fact that above his private ideas, there is a world of absolute ideas according to which he must shape his own; he catches a glimpse of a whole intellectual kingdom in which he participates, but which is greater than he. This is the first intuition of the realm of truth. From the moment when he first becomes conscious of these higher ideas, he sets himself to scrutinizing their nature; he asks whence these pre-eminent representations hold their prerogatives and, in so far as he believes that he has discovered their causes, he undertakes to put these causes into action for himself, in order that he may draw from them by his own force the effects which they produce; that is to say, he attributes to himself the right of making concepts. Thus the faculty of conception has individualized itself. But to understand its origins and function, it must be attached to the social conditions upon which it depends.

It may be objected that we show the concept in one of its aspects only, and that its unique role is not the assuring of a harmony among minds, but also, and to a greater extent, their harmony with the nature of things. It seems as though it had a reason for existence only on condition of being true, that is to say, objective, and as though its impersonality were only a consequence of its objectivity. It is in regard to things, thought of as adequately as possible, that minds ought to communicate. Nor do we deny that the evolution of concepts has been partially in this direction. The concept which was first held as true because it was collective tends to be no longer collective except on condition of being held as true:

we demand its credentials of it before according it our confidence. But we must not lose sight of the fact that even to-day the great majority of the concepts which we use are not methodically constituted; we get them from language, that is to say, from common experience, without submitting them to any criticism. The scientifically elaborated and criticized concepts are always in the very slight minority. Also, between them and those which draw all their authority from the fact that they are collective, there are only differences of degree. A collective representation presents guarantees of objectivity by the fact that it is collective: for it is not without sufficient reason that it has been able to generalize and maintain itself with persistence. If it were out of accord with the nature of things, it would never have been able to acquire an extended and prolonged empire over intellects. At bottom, the confidence inspired by scientific concepts is due to the fact that they can be methodically controlled. But a collective representation is necessarily submitted to a control that is repeated indefinitely; the men who accept it verify it by their own experience. Therefore, it could not be wholly inadequate for its subject. It is true that it may express this by means of imperfect symbols; but scientific symbols themselves are never more than approximative. It is precisely this principle which is at the basis of the method which we follow in the study of religious phenomena: we take it as an axiom that religious beliefs, howsoever strange their appearance may be at times, contain a truth which must be discovered.

On the other hand, it is not at all true that concepts, even when constructed according to the rules of science, get their authority uniquely from their objective value. It is not enough that they be true to be believed. If they are not in harmony with the other beliefs and opinions, or, in a word, with the mass of the other collective representations, they will be denied; minds will be closed to them; consequently it will be as though they did not exist. To-day it is generally sufficient that they bear the stamp of science to receive a sort of privileged credit, because we have faith in science. But this faith does not differ essentially from religious faith. In the last resort, the value which we attribute to science depends upon the idea which we collectively form of its nature and role in life; that is as much as to say that it expresses a state of public opinion. In all social life, in fact, science rests upon opinion. It is undoubtedly true that this opinion can be taken as the object of a study and a science made of it; this is what sociology principally consists in. But the science of opinion does not make opinions; it can only observe them and make them more conscious of themselves. It is true that by this means it can lead them to change, but science continues to be dependent upon opinion at the very moment when it seems to be making its laws; for, as we have already shown, it is from opinion that it holds the force necessary to act upon opinion.

Saying that concepts express the manner in which society represents things is also saying that conceptual thought is coeval with humanity itself. We refuse to see in it the product of a more or less retarded culture. A man who did not think with concepts would not be a man, for he would not be a social being. If reduced to having only individual perceptions, he would be indistinguishable from the beasts. If it has been possible to sustain the contrary thesis, it is because concepts have been defined by characteristics which are not essential to them. They have been identified with general ideas and with clearly limited and circumscribed general ideas. In these conditions it has possibly seemed as though the inferior societies had no concepts properly so called; for they have only rudimentary processes of generalization and the ideas which they use are not generally very well defined. But the greater part of our concepts are equally indetermined; we force ourselves to define them only in discussions or when doing careful work. We have also seen that conceiving is not generalizing. Thinking conceptually is not simply isolating and grouping together the common characteristics of a certain number of objects; it is relating the variable to the permanent, the individual to the social. And since logical thought commences with the concept, it follows that it has always existed; there is no period in history when men have lived in a chronic confusion and contradiction. To be sure, we cannot insist too much upon the different characteristics which logic presents at different periods in history; it develops like the societies themselves. But howsoever real these differences may be, they should not cause us to neglect the similarities, which are no less essential.

IV   We are now in a position to take up a final question which has already been raised in our introduction and which has been taken as understood in the remainder of this work. We have seen that at least some of the categories are social things. The question is where they got this character.

Undoubtedly it will be easily understood that since they are themselves concepts, they are the work of the group. It can even be said that there are no other concepts which present to an equal degree the signs by which a collective representation is recognized. In fact, their stability and impersonality are such that they have often passed as being absolutely universal and immutable. Also, as they express the fundamental conditions for an agreement between minds, it seems evident that they have been elaborated by society.

But the problem concerning them is more complex, for they are social in another sense and, as it were in the second degree. They not only come from society, but the things which they express are of a social nature. Not only is it society which has founded them, but their contents are the different aspects of the social being: the category of class was at first indistinct from the concept of the human group; it is the rhythm of social life which is at the basis of the category of time; the territory occupied by the society furnished the material for the category of space; it is the collective force which was the prototype of the concept of efficient force, an essential element in the category of causality. However, the categories are not made to be applied only to the social realm; they reach out to all reality. Then how is it that they have taken from society the models upon which they have been constructed?

It is because they are the pre-eminent concepts, which have a preponderating part in our knowledge. In fact, the function of the categories is to dominate and envelop all the other concepts: they are permanent moulds for the mental life. Now for them to embrace such an object, they must be founded upon a reality of equal amplitude.

Undoubtedly the relations which they express exist in an implicit way in individual consciousnesses. The individual lives in time, and, as we have said, he has a certain sense of temporal orientation. He is situated at a determined point in space, and it has even been held, and sustained with good reasons, that all sensations have something special about them. He has a feeling of resemblances; similar representations are brought together and the new representation formed by their union has a sort of generic character. We also have the sensation of a certain regularity in the order of the succession of phenomena; even an animal is not incapable of this. However, all these relations are strictly personal for the individual who recognizes them, and consequently the notion of them which he may have can in no case go beyond his own narrow horizon. The generic images which are formed in my consciousness by the fusion of similar images represent only the objects which I have perceived directly; there is nothing there which could give me the idea of a class, that is to say, of a mould including the *whole* group of all possible objects which satisfy the same condition. Also, it would be necessary to have the idea of group in the first place, and the mere observations of our interior life could never awaken that in us. But, above all, there is no individual experience, howsoever extended and prolonged it may be, which could give a suspicion of the existence of a whole class which would embrace every single being, and to which other classes are only co-ordinated or subordinated species. This idea of *all,* which is at the basis of the classifications which we have just cited, could not have come from the individual himself, who is only a part in relation to the whole and who never attains more than an infinitesimal fraction of reality. And yet there is perhaps no other category of greater importance; for as the role of the categories is to envelop all the other concepts, the category *par excellence* would seem to be this very concept of *totality*. The theorists of knowledge ordinarily postulate it is if it came of itself, while it really surpasses the contents of each individual consciousness taken alone to an infinite degree.

For the same reasons, the space which I know by my senses, of which I am the centre and where everything is disposed in relation to me, could not be space in general, which contains all extensions and where these are co-ordinated by personal guide-lines which are common to everybody. In the same way, the concrete duration which I feel passing within me and with me could not give me the idea of time in general: the first expresses only the rhythm of my individual life; the second should correspond to the rhythm of a life which is not that of any individual in particular, but in which all participate. In the same way, finally, the regularities which I am able to conceive in the manner in which my sensations succeed one another may well have a value for me; they explain how it comes about that when I am given the first of two phenomena whose concurrence I have observed, I tend to expect the other. But this personal state of expectation could not be confounded with the conception of a universal order of succession which imposes itself upon all minds and all events.

Since the world expressed by the entire system of concepts is the one that society regards, society alone can furnish the most general notions with which it should be represented. Such an object can be embraced only by a subject which contains all the individual subjects within it. Since the universe does not exist except in so far as it is thought of, and since it is not completely thought of except by society, it takes a place in this latter; it becomes a part of society's interior life, while this is the totality, outside of which nothing exists. The concept of totality is only the abstract form of the concept of society: it is the whole which includes all things, the supreme class which embraces all other classes. Such is the final principle upon which repose all these primitive classifications where beings from every realm are placed and classified in social forms, exactly like men. But if the world is inside of society, the space which this latter occupies becomes confounded with space in general. In fact, we have seen how each thing has its assigned place in social space, and the degree to which this space in general differs from the concrete expanses which we perceive is well shown by the fact that this localization is wholly ideal and in no way resembles what it would have been if it had been dictated to us by sensuous experience alone. For the same reason, the rhythm of collective life dominates and embraces the varied rhythms of all the elementary lives from which it results; consequently the time which it expresses dominates and embraces all particular durations. It is time in general. For a long time the history of the world has been only another aspect of the history of society. The one commences with the other; the periods of the first are determined by the periods of the second. This impersonal and total duration is measured, and the guide-lines in

relation to which it is divided and organized are fixed
by the movements of concentration or dispersion of society; or, more generally, the periodical necessities for a
collective renewal. If these critical instants are generally
attached to some material phenomenon, such as the
regular recurrence of such or such a star or the alterna-
tion of the seasons, it is because objective signs are necessary to make this essentially social organization intelligible to all. In the same way, finally, the causal relation, from the moment when it is collectively stated by
the group, becomes independent of every individual
consciousness; it rises above all particular minds and
events. It is a law whose value depends upon no person.
We have already shown how it is clearly thus that it
seems to have originated.

Another reason explains why the constituent elements of the categories should have been taken from
social life: it is because the relations which they express
could not have been learned except in and through society. If they are in a sense immanent in the life of an individual, he has neither a reason nor the means for
learning them, reflecting upon them and forming them
into distinct idea. In order to orient himself personally
in space and to know at what moments he should satisfy his various organic needs, he has no need of making,
once and for all, a conceptual representation of time
and space. Many animals are able to find the road
which leads to places with which they are familiar; they
come back at a proper moment without knowing any of
the categories; sensations are enough to direct them automatically. They would also be enough for men, if
their sensations had to satisfy only individual needs.
To recognize the fact that one thing resembles another
which we have already experienced, it is in no way necessary that we arrange them all in groups and species:
the way in which similar images call up each other and
unite is enough to give the feeling of resemblance. The
impression that a certain thing has already been seen or

experienced implies no classification. To recognize the things which we should seek or from which we should flee, it would not be necessary to attach the effects of the two to their causes by a logical bond, if individual conveniences were the only ones in question. Purely empirical sequences and strong connections between the concrete representations would be as sure guides for the will. Not only is it true that the animal has no others, but also our own personal conduct frequently supposes nothing more. The prudent man is the one who has a very clear sensation of what must be done, but which he would ordinarily be quite incapable of stating as a general law.

It is a different matter with society. This is possible only when the individuals and things which compose it are divided into certain groups, that is to say, classified, and when these groups are classified in relation to each other. Society supposes a self-conscious organization which is nothing other than a classification. This organization of society naturally extends itself to the place which this occupies. To avoid all collisions, it is necessary that each particular group have a determined portion of space assigned to it: in other terms, it is necessary that space in general be divided, differentiated, arranged, and that these divisions and arrangements be known to everybody. On the other hand, every summons to a celebration, a hunt or a military expedition implies fixed and established dates, and consequently that a common time is agreed upon, which everybody conceives in the same fashion. Finally, the co-operation of many persons with the same end in view is possible only when they are in agreement as to the relation which exists between this end and the means of attaining it, that is to say, when the same causal relation is admitted by all the co-operators in the enterprise. It is not surprising, therefore, that social time, social space, social classes and causality should be the basis of the corresponding categories, since it is under their social forms that these different relations were first grasped with a certain clarity by the human intellect.

In summing up, then, we must say that society is not at all the illogical or a-logical, incoherent and fantastic being which it has too often been considered. Quite on the contrary, the collective consciousness is the highest form of the psychic life, since it is the consciousness of the consciousnesses. Being placed outside of and above individual and local contingencies, it sees things only in their permanent and essential aspects, which it crystallizes into communicable ideas. At the very same time that it sees from above, it sees farther; at every moment of time, it embraces all known reality; that is why it alone can furnish the mind with the moulds which are applicable to the totality of things and which make it possible to think of them. It does not create these moulds artificially; it finds them within itself; it does nothing but become conscious of them. They translate the ways of being which are found in all the stages of reality but which appear in their full clarity only at the summit, because the extreme complexity of the psychic life which passes there necessitates a greater development of consciousness. Attributing social origins to logical thought is not debasing it or diminishing its value or reducing it to nothing more than a system of artificial combinations; on the contrary, it is relating it to a cause which implies it naturally. But this is not saying that the ideas elaborated in this way are at once adequate for their object. If society is something universal in relation to the individual, it is none the less an individuality itself, which has its own personal physiognomy and its idiosyncrasies; it is a particular subject and consequently particularizes whatever it thinks of. Therefore collective representations also contain subjective elements, and these must be progressively rooted out, if we are to approach reality more closely. But howsoever crude these may have been at the beginning, the fact remains that with them the germ of a new mentality was given, to which the individual could never have raised himself by his own efforts: by them the way was opened to a stable, impersonal and organized thought which then had nothing to do except to develop its nature.

Also, the causes which have determined this development do not seem to be specifically different from those which gave it its initial impulse. If logical thought tends to rid itself more and more of the subjective and personal elements which it still retains from its origin, it is not because extra-social factors have intervened; it is much rather because a social life of a new sort is developing. It is this international life which has already resulted in universalizing religious beliefs. As it extends, the collective horizon enlarges; the society ceases to appear as the only whole, to become a part of a much vaster one, with indetermined frontiers, which is susceptible of advancing indefinitely. Consequently things can no longer be contained in the social moulds according to which they were primitively classified; they must be organized according to principles which are their own, so logical organization differentiates itself from the social organization and becomes autonomous. Really and truly human thought is not a primitive fact; it is the product of history; it is the ideal limit towards which we are constantly approaching, but which in all probability we shall never succeed in reaching.

Thus, it is not at all true that between science on the one hand, and morals and religion on the other, there exists that sort of antinomy which has so frequently been admitted, for the two forms of human activity really come from one and the same source. Kant understood this very well, and therefore he made the speculative reason and the practical reason two different aspects of the same faculty. According to him, what makes their unity is the fact that the two are directed towards the universal. Rational thinking is thinking according to the laws which are imposed upon all reasonable beings; acting morally is conducting one's self according to those maxims which can be extended without contradiction to all wills. In other words, science and morals imply that the individual is capable of raising himself above his own peculiar point of view and of living an impersonal life. In fact, it cannot be doubted that this is a trait common to all the higher forms of thought and action. What Kant's system does not explain, however, is the origin of this sort of contradiction which is realized in man. Why is he forced to do violence to himself by leaving his individuality, and, inversely, why is the impersonal law obliged to be dissipated by incarnating itself in individuals? Is it answered that there are two antagonistic worlds in which we participate equally, the world of matter and sense on the one hand, and the world of pure and impersonal reason on the other? That is merely repeating the question in slightly different terms, for what we are trying to find out is why we must lead these two existences at the same time. Why do these two worlds, which seem to contradict each other, not remain outside of each other, and why must they mutually penetrate one another in spite of their antagonism? The only explanation which has ever been given of this singular necessity is the hypothesis of the Fall, with all the difficulties which it implies, and which need not be repeated here. On the other hand, all mystery disappears the moment that it is recognized that impersonal reason is only another name given to collective thought. For this is possible only through a group of individuals; it supposes them, and in their turn, they suppose it, for they can continue to exist only by grouping themselves together. The kingdom of ends and impersonal truths can realize itself only by the cooperation of particular wills, and the reasons for which these participate in it are the same as those for which they co-operate. In a word, there is something social in all of us, and since social life embraces at once both representations and practices, this impersonality naturally extends to ideas as well as to acts.

Perhaps some will be surprised to see us connect the most elevated forms of thought with society: the cause appears quite humble, in consideration of the value which we attribute to the effect. Between the world of the senses and appetites on the one hand, and that of reason and morals on the other, the distance is so considerable that the second would seem to have been able to add itself to the first only by a creative act. But attributing to society this preponderating role in the genesis of our nature is not denying this creation; for society has a creative power which no other observable being can equal. In fact, all creation, if not a mystical operation which escapes science and knowledge, is the product of a synthesis. Now if the synthesis of particular conceptions which take place in each individual consciousness are already and of themselves productive of novelties, how much more efficacious these vast syntheses of complete consciousnesses which make society must be! A society is the most powerful combination of physical and moral forces of which nature offers us an example. Nowhere else is an equal richness of different materials, carried to such a degree of concentration, to be found. Then it is not surprising that a higher life disengages itself which, by reacting upon the elements of which it is the product, raises them to a higher plane of existence and transforms them.

Thus sociology appears destined to open a new way to the science of man. Up to the present, thinkers were placed before this double alternative: either explain the superior and specific faculties of men by connecting them to the inferior forms of his being, the reason to the senses, or the mind to matter, which is equivalent to denying their uniqueness; or else attach them to some super-experimental reality which was postulated, but whose existence could be established by no observation. What put them in this difficulty was the fact that the individual passed as being the *finis naturæ*—the ultimate creation of nature; it seemed that there was nothing beyond him, or at least nothing that science could touch. But from the moment when it is recognized that above the individual there is society, and that this is not a nominal being created by reason, but a system of active forces, a new manner of explaining men becomes possible. To conserve his distinctive traits it is no longer necessary to put them outside experience. At least, before going to this last extremity, it would be well to see if that which surpasses the individual, though it is within him, does not come from this super-individual reality which we experience in society. To be sure, it cannot be said at present to what point these explanations may be able to reach, and whether or not they are of a nature to resolve all the problems. But it is equally impossible to mark in advance a limit beyond which they cannot go. What must be done is to try the hypothesis and submit it as methodically as possible to the control of facts. This is what we have tried to do.

A Study of History   ARNOLD J. TOYNBEE

Abridged by D. C. Somervell

TWO HANDSOME PAPERBACK VOLUMES
IN A BEAUTIFULLY DESIGNED SLIP COVER

Now—Dell presents the long-awaited two-volume abridgement of Toynbee's monumental masterpiece, which *The New York Times* has called, ". . . unquestionably one of the great works of our times."

This remarkably concise abridgement is the work of D. C. Somervell who, with marvelous skill, has retained all of Toynbee's immense depth and breadth of thought. He has managed to preserve not only its texture and atmosphere, but—for the most part—the author's own words.

Two-volume boxed set $1.95